*T*urning *P*oint

A Tribute Memoir
Told through the Voices of Those Who Knew
Peter A. Gallione
July 9, 1946 - October 31, 2020

Compiled, Written, and Edited by
Annmarie Gallione
and
Eve Jensen
Cover Design by Nathaniel Jensen

Copyright © 2021 Annmarie Gallione
ISBN Paperback: 978-1-09839-238-3

"Always make as many friends as you can."
\- *Peter Gallione*
February 6, 1974

We acknowledge and thank all of those who contributed to this memoir, and to Peter's life.

TABLE OF CONTENTS

INTRODUCTION

By Annmarie Gallione

For all who implored him, my father never did write his life story.

His was a life that may be better told from the perspective of others, in any event. Some knew him from when he was an adorable and charming "altar boy", raised in a loving and secure home. Those with some misfortune encountered him as a criminal and an addict, prone to selfishness, violence, and substance abuse. Many crossed my father's path in one of his drug programs and now have him to thank, in part, for their own recovery. Still others were deeply connected to him as a husband, a family member, and a friend. Until the day that he died, he remained a counselor, confidant, and loved one to so, so many. Once he overcame his drug addiction, relationships became everything to my father and defined his world. His was quite the journey, and I invite you to read the words and listen to the voices of those who encountered him along the way.

As his only child ("that we know of", we often joked), I have always maintained a unique vantage point in my father's life. He spent 3 years of my early life in prison, yet our parent-child bond was as impenetrable as the walls that kept him in. Despite a good amount of physical distance between us in my childhood, our connection remained deep and vast. I most certainly was "of him", even though my mother was my primary — and often sole — parent. For reasons beyond any of our understanding, my mother often had to admit that I was my "father's daughter", both on the surface and underneath.

My mother could have — but did not — alienate me from my father. When he was incarcerated from 1973 until 1976, we regularly visited him "at work"; he spent his furlough weekends "at home" with us and the letter correspondence between my father and my mother (and me) was honest and plentiful. My mother saved 115 letters from my father from December of 1973 until August of 1976, each written in his beautiful penmanship, and their contents provide a wealth of insight into how his incarceration impacted him. That collection of letters deserves its own volume, but suffice it to say that my parents' regular correspondence and our family visits during that time frame kept my relationship with my father alive. It may also have kept him alive, as some of his writings suggest.

As a child, I was well aware that my father had led a wayward existence in his youth and that the New Jersey criminal justice system had succeeded — with him — in its endeavor to rehabilitate. I also knew that my mother and virtually every other member of my family still loved him, transgressions notwithstanding. Most significantly, I never once felt disconnected from him and I always felt deeply loved by him. I came to learn more specifics as I grew older — the drugs, the women, the fighting, lord, the fighting. My father eventually took full responsibility for it all and that gave him the power to change. In my belief, it also gave him the power to help others change themselves. He took ownership of the insecurities that fed his addiction, accepted responsibility for his misconduct, served his time, and took a sharp right out of the darkness and into the light, never going back. And many others followed.

When he was released and made the wise decision to move away from North Jersey and New York City, my mother allowed me to visit my father for weeks at a time without her. Until she died in 1983, my father's mother and I frequently visited him together in South Jersey. There, I got to see him work firsthand, with kids not that much older than me who had committed crimes as a result of substance abuse. He often made the 90-minute drive north to see me, sometimes just to watch one of my games, and for most special occasions. He was a big "phone talker", as many of those reading this surely know, and I likely spoke more to him from a distance than I would have if I had lived with him. It didn't hurt that he was incredibly easy to talk to. During these years, my father devoted an immense amount of his energy to his career and to implementing and administering the kind of care — not punishment — that he believed that addicts deserved.

At the age of 16, when my own life took a slightly wild and dangerous turn, I learned firsthand what it was like to be counseled one-on-one on addiction by my father. There were many hours of honest discussion, lots of education and certainly a good amount of frustration, fear, and tears. There was also a behind-the-scenes "scared straight" tour of the women's prison, which was an interesting experience for a 16-year-old, sexuality-questioning girl and probably did not have the effect that my father intended.

Surely my father was going to do everything in his power to ensure that I took a different path than he took. I will never, ever forget the look of combined anger, disappointment, breathlessness, fear, and love on his face when he stormed through the front door of my mother's house on Westside Avenue that late summer night in 1987, after learning that his daughter had been using cocaine, his own drug of choice in his youth.

I thought I was quite convincing in my arguments: I was a 4-year varsity athlete, a successful student, and a socially well-adjusted and respectful kid who just happened to be "responsibly" using drugs. Ordinary life was kind of boring, I claimed, so what was the real harm if I could manage it all? To my dad, with his past and his own addiction, this was his worst fear and his most egregious failure. The problem was that he *knew* that what I was saying was true. He had experienced the same feelings that I described to him when I used drugs, and it scared the hell out of him.

My father's approach to substance abuse treatment could (and does) span volumes. One of the most successful achievements that he often mentioned, and of which he was very proud, was that he "*wrote the juvenile drug treatment program for the entire State of New Jersey*". Whether or not he gave himself too much credit, the fact is that the self-bestowed accolade gave him street cred that I assume helped his success in treating others and administering drug programs for decades. He was the addict-turned-treatment provider, and his approach worked.

***

By Tyrone Johnson

I met Pete in 1976 or 1977 at a substance abuse program called Turning Point, located in Camden County, New Jersey. He was a cocky 31 year-old Italian outpatient Counselor, running the outpatient unit. I was a cocky 26 year-old Black Muslim senior client in the residential program. I had grown up in the Italian area of Camden so I thought I knew something of his culture. I had become somewhat comfortable with grouping and program life after having been there for eighteen months, and had earned work release status. I was working as a house framing assistant, planning on returning to my home in Camden.

During this time, Turning Point was in transition from being a small program in a residential house to becoming a large 30-bed unit in a brand new building. I remained in the program throughout this transition, becoming a trusted senior in the program dedicated to changing my life. In a conversation with a couple of the staff in the program about my future, there was a suggestion I might be able to get a job as a counselor assistant in this new program administration that would be taking over. I had heard that it would be Pete Gallione from the outpatient unit who would be the administrator.

I didn't think I had a chance in hell to be hired. I had no college background and the only experience I had was from having been through the program. The staff there had me pumped, so I said the worst that can happen is he says no, and I applied.

When I went to Pete's office, my hands were sweating bad. I was nervous, so as I went to shake his hand, I drew my hand up my pants to take some of the sweat off. That was the beginning of our beautiful and lifelong friendship. To the day he passed, we used to laugh about that interview. Pete, being Pete, would say "I knew you was scared as shit, trying to wipe that sweat off your hand."

From that day to this, I have found Peter A. Gallione to be a man's man, and a better friend. A "man's man" is a man that other men look to and have no problem following. That's my Friend and Brother.

After working together for a short period and becoming friends, I realized how intelligent and dedicated he was to what he was putting together at Turning Point. He truly invested all of himself in what he believed and that program became one of the most influential and renowned programs in the state. Pete became one of the more sought-after authorities on substance abuse in New Jersey.

I attribute my success and where I'm at today to him. Because he was always straightforward and honest, if I was wrong or short he would bring it to me. The most impactful experience was one day early in our friendship. He came to me and said, "Listen Hamin, this whole thing [meaning Turning Point] is getting ready to take off. I'll take you with me but I won't carry you, you need to prepare yourself for this ride, be committed, and go to school", which I did.

I grew to love him as a friend and brother. When his brother Philip passed, I found my way there to support him, and when mine passed he found his way through Camden to support me. It was the same when our mothers passed. Pete introduced me to Klaus and Ann Aschim, who were his close friends and became close and trusted friends of mine also. Pete introduced me to my current wife of 36 years and my two children call him Uncle Pete. This man had more influence in my life than my father or brother did.

I know for a fact not only did this man impact me this way, but there are so many others that have similar stories to tell. Pete had a heart as big as the world and that made him so much fun to be around. He had a way of picking at you where you felt and, as he often said, "he may not be right, but he ain't never wrong." With sports he was the biggest New York fan, anything New York, and you couldn't out-talk him on much if he really wanted to mess with you. Early in our friendship we would play basketball, football, bowling and he was good at softball, not me. He was very competitive in life and sports, sometimes to the point of, "Ok Pete, I don't want to hear it."

Then there were those real moments when we talked of wrongs, rights and could have/should haves in our lives. He was easy to talk to and share with; he had a profound way of not being judgmental or condemning, which I think came from his protective side, because that was just as strong as that competitive nature in him. He didn't have a problem with having to fight if that's what needed to happen. Don't get it wrong, he was a bull physically and family meant everything to him, and he didn't have a problem letting you know that!

Over our forty-something year friendship, this part of our bio speaks to his transitions and accomplishments. Through our many, many conversations I found that Pete and I both grew up as knot heads, meaning that through our selfishness we both ended up in situations that landed him in prison and me on my way to prison!

Pete told me that he volunteered to go into a substance abuse program in prison by the name of Alpha-Meta, originally for its school and work release program. After going through the program, he found it working for him, and there he met others who became close friends and mentors to each other. Pete became an administrator in the program and completed his BA degree.

Upon his release from prison, Pete relocated to South Jersey, going to work with adult substance abusers. This is where I was befriended by Pete. Through our strong and close relationship and friendship, together our lives and accomplishments blew up! As stated above, Pete became the Administrator of Turning Point Residential and Outpatient Substance Abuse Program. Achieving Joint Commission of Hospital Accreditation, which is known as JCI-Accreditation, was a profound accomplishment for Pete; he was one of the first, if not the first, to achieve this accreditation for Substance Abuse Programs in New Jersey. He stayed in the Adult Substance Abuse field for approximately ten years, I left about two or three years before he did to pursue my own business in home improvements and remodeling.

Pete decided that he also wanted to pursue a lifelong dream to open a hot dog business, which he called PUPP's. He built this business from the floor up, acquiring an empty new storefront which he remodeled to what he wanted. The store opened and did well for a while, then business fell off, and he went into Juvenile Correction addressing the issue of substance abuse within the young adult community.

Life's changes had forced me back into a more stable work environment, so I applied for a job at Camden House, a Juvenile Residential Program under the NJ Department of Corrections. My experience and training under Pete in Reality Based Therapy and Counseling allowed me to quickly move up the ladder. This department was also in transition to a more therapeutic approach to juvenile issues within the correction system. Pete came into the Juvenile Program, first developing and administering the Camden Day Program for youth as an alternative to detention. It was there that Pete realized that the majority of these juvenile corrections problems stemmed from substance abuse issues within their communities. So he brought it to another close friend who had gone through the program with him and they took it to Correction administrators. This began Pete's twenty-year career in Juvenile Justice.

Pete managed to build the first Juvenile Substance Abuse Community-based program in Camden County from the ground up. In this program, Pete introduced his residents to the horticulture trade, to the point that the program developed a thriving business and apprenticeship.

Pete was always bullish in his approach to substance abuse. Between this and his legitimate knowledge in the field, he was afforded the opportunity to develop and build a department within Juvenile Justice to oversee program development throughout the State. I can't tell you the number of awards and accommodations he received for the work he did in the field of Substance Abuse Treatment and Programing. As said in the athletic circle, the man was a Beast!

He didn't die in my heart. I hear him all the time, "Hamin, when you coming down?? "

***

If not for my father's experience and expertise, the substance abuse journey to recovery for many would likely have been vastly different. To him, it started with identifying the emotional source that sparked addiction within the people he was treating. The earlier in someone's life that it was recognized, the better. In one of his many letters to my mother and I from prison, this one dated January 28, 1975, he stated: *"I really get a feeling of self-worth by doing things with kids."* He was 28 years old and had just returned from a speaking engagement at a local high school as part of his drug program during incarceration. Through Alpha-Meta, my father found his home working with juveniles. This discovery is also likely why he was successful at detouring his own daughter away from a life led by addiction. The stories of those varied, young individuals who he helped over the years are extremely compelling, and I greatly look forward to hearing more about them and to perhaps writing about them one day.[1]

My connection to my father became even stronger during my years in college and law school, when our conversations turned deep and philosophical and when he became comfortable discussing his past with me without any filters. My father and I were nothing if not brutally honest with each other in those conversations. I am sure that there are some things that we chose not to tell one another, but not many.

During law school, I moved in with him for a summer and we grew even closer. We spent every Wednesday in Atlantic City, each week at a different casino, enjoying dinner and some interesting conversation and then beating the casinos at Blackjack. We "took 'em", my dad would say, because we won each of those nights. I haven't gambled since that

---

[1] If my father helped you, and you would ever like to share your story, please email me at annmariegallione@gmail.com.

summer and will die a winner, just as I like to think my father did. I eventually utilized one of his connections, took a job, and settled myself and my family in South Jersey, very near to where he lived. My relationship with my father never stopped growing and thriving, and hence I am endlessly grateful for his recovery.

Certain people have an energy that is like a gravitational pull, and my father was one of them. Early in his life, his energy was largely the product of insecurity, frustration, and weakness masked as strength. Later, after a whole lot of internal work, honesty, and acceptance, my father developed a "presence" about him, the positive kind that stays with you long after he has left. People just liked being around him. His smile lit up a room and, well, those dimples… they unquestionably got him (and me) out of some prett-*y* stick-*y* situations.

What I may not have realized during my father's lifetime is how profoundly his loss would be felt when he died, not just by me, but by so very many people. People who felt that they owed their life to him, people who still relied on him regularly for counsel and for guidance, even well into his retirement. People who loved him (two of whom had married and divorced him), learned from him, laughed with him, and felt so blessed to have been connected to him. The outpouring of support from these individuals, and my realization that his loss was not mine alone, eventually led me here, to this project and these pages.

My father died on October 31, 2020 under a full moon, in the throes of a worldwide pandemic, in the midst of a national racial reckoning, and during a presidency that was likely a contributing factor to his troubled heart. He had repeatedly said that he wanted to go out with "that big one" at the end, and so it was. He got his wish. And we all simultaneously got a punch in the gut.

This tribute and collection were my best attempt to "memorialize" my father during a time when traditional memorials were unsafe and when they placed individual and public health at risk. A service in his honor, during a time when hugging — one of my father's trademarks — was discouraged and dangerous, was not an option when he passed. Instead, I have offered those who knew him a way to honor and celebrate him more permanently by thinking of him, writing about him, and contributing here. I am so appreciative of those who did. Your essays have made us laugh, cry, ponder, and appreciate. Without them, we would not continue to feel my father's presence and impact as deeply as we still do. Your memories of him are now forever etched in our hearts and minds, and his legacy continues.

To provide context, we have shared some backstory to accompany the essays and to give those who have chosen to take this journey with us a better sense of dates, times, places, and events. Where there was a "ghostwriter", it is noted. Where spoken words were captured, every effort was made to transcribe them accurately. Only small edits were made to submissions in order to preserve the voice and sentiment of those who contributed.

I have so much gratitude for my children, Eve and Nathaniel, who were an immense source of pride for their grandfather and who helped me create this work. And to my mother, Mary, who was the true conduit for my close relationship with my father and who soldiered on day after day despite her own personal pain and anguish and nurtured the relationship between a father and his daughter nonetheless.

If you knew my father during his unpredictable lifetime, thank you for being a part of his world. I promise you, he appreciated you. If you did not, I hope that the story of his life illustrates that rehabilitation, recovery and redemption are indeed possible and that, in the end, all that truly matters is love.

***

PART ONE
THE EARLY YEARS

Baby Peter with his mom and dad, ~1947

The home that my father was born into on July 9, 1946 was drenched in love. My grandmother, Ellen ("Ellie Pooh"), was the epitome of unconditional adoration. She created an ever-present atmosphere of acceptance for her children and grandchildren, and that environment may ultimately have been what formed the foundation for my father's later success in rehabilitation. Her warmth, and the comfort that she provided to her family, instilled a goodness in my father that, while temporarily clouded by addiction and diminished during his adolescence, prevailed in the end. I was fortunate to know this unconditional love and acceptance directly from my father's mother and to share a unique and special bond with her throughout my childhood. Where my father was absent, his mother was fully and wholly present in my life, teaching me how important goodness and humanity are. When my father eventually overcame his insecurities and his addiction, this same goodness and humanity guided his later life.

Peter was the second son born to Ellen and Philip ("Nip" to pretty much everyone). His older brother, Philip, was born on June 9, 1942, four years and one month before my father. Nip was one of eight children — Joseph "Joey", Philip "Philly/Nip", Peter "Petey", Alexander "Sonny", Lillian "Lizzie", Julia, Esther, and Francesca "Francie" — born into a loving and boisterous Italian family: the Galliones. I never met Nip, since he passed away early in 1971 while my mother was pregnant with me. My mother tells me that Grandpa Nip was the first person after her to feel me move during her pregnancy, and that this occurred from the hospital on the day that he died. As I came to understand the type of person Nip was throughout my life, I somewhat convinced myself that his soul had left his body in January of 1971 and entered my own just a few months later. (Prove me wrong.)

Left to right: Petey, Sonny, Joey, Philly; Francie, Lizzie, Julia, Esther

One of the few things that could bring my father down was his belief, later in life, that he had been a cause of stress for his parents. He did not live with regret, exactly, but he did feel deep remorse for the troubles he caused them during his youth. There was usually a change in his facial expressions and in his tone of voice whenever he recalled how good both of his parents were and how much pain he believed that he had caused them. His father died when he was off the rails in 1971, but his mother did live to see him turn his life around and, to him, this was an incredible blessing.

My father used to storytell about the emigration of our ancestors from Italy, and the history (in his mind) went a bit like this: in Naples, Italy, the family had the surname Gaglione and those who journeyed to the United States did so, in part, to distance themselves from a violent and troublesome contingent back home. Those who left their home in Italy desired a fresh life and a separation from the havoc-wreaking family that remained. Essentially, the "good ones" came to America. Not wanting to be associated with the Gagliones, when the first of them arrived at Ellis Island (in some year that I wish I knew), there was rumored to be a conscious effort to drop the "g" and add an "l", thus creating a similar but distinct last name for the family. Surely, it could also have been a typographical error, as was common at Ellis Island, but my father much preferred the made-for-movie version. The theoretical history also provided him with some cover to explain why he, himself, was prone to a violent and turbulent decade during his teens and early twenties. If he was genetically predisposed to cause trouble, he thought, then how was he supposed to avoid it?

Sometime in the late 1940s, Philip and Ellen made a big decision. Nip, being a tremendous lover of fun and games, had a dream of opening a bowling alley. Another family member, Nena, had married a Mexican citizen and moved to Mexico City, where she raised a beautiful and loving family of her own.

So, Nip packed up his adoring wife and two young sons and trekked from New Jersey to Mexico City. A dreamer, he was. Not much is known about my father's family's time in Mexico; however, years later, he would form a bond with our family there that prompted several international visits, weekly telephone/video conversations, and an extremely deep kinship. From my vantage point, it appeared that our cousin from Mexico, Jaime, replaced the brother that my father had lost when he was only 35 years old.

***

By Jaime Gerner Alonso

Spoken in English and Spanish from Mexico City, transcribed by Annmarie

My grandmother had met my grandfather back in the States at a bar he owned in Englewood, New Jersey. They made wine and it was clandestine. My grandmother was only 15 years old when they met. They lived in Manhattan and had a little restaurant. My grandfather was a chef at the restaurant and also worked for the government building the highway to Alaska. Lizzie worked in the little restaurant named "Port Vigo" which was on 60th Street and 5th Avenue.

Lillian was their only daughter and they called her "Nena", my mother. She was born in Englewood and moved to Mexico City with my grandparents when she was 17. My father was an American football coach and met my mother at the bus stop near the furniture store that my grandparents managed. They didn't want my mom to marry him so they sent her back to New York with her aunts. My father, who loved her very much, organized a football match in New York with his team against a high school, only because he wanted to see her again. It was a lovely story.

My grandmother, Lizzie, came here in 1948. My grandfather was Spanish from Spain. They saved a lot of money from him working on the highway to Alaska, and they moved to Mexico City to run a furniture store. My grandmother and my grandfather manufactured and sold furniture and they also managed a bowling alley and a big restaurant. They had the very first bowling alley in Mexico City, called "Boliches Zago". I remember the address downtown: 18 Tacuba. My grandparents received cousin Peter's family who lived there and worked all together for 2 years and they went back to New Jersey.

Peter, who was 2 years old, and his family came by train or by car. They stayed for about 2 years in Mexico City. Cousin Philip could speak Spanish because he was old enough and went to school.

I went to Brooklyn when my grandmother died in 1981. While there, cousin Philip gave my mother a teddy bear promising that he would go to visit her in Mexico soon. He never did, so the teddy bear was Nena's companion forever. I still have it to this day. I keep the teddy bear in our guest room here in Mexico City and when cousin Peter ("primo") came to visit us not long ago, he and the teddy bear became friends and he slept in the room with him. We thought this was special and comical since Nena had been given the bear by Peter's brother in New York and here was cousin Peter sleeping in the room with it.

I miss my primo, Peter, very much. He was very special to me.

***

By Lena Jacks

Spoken by Lena, written by Annmarie

My mother, Francie, was Nip's sister and Peter's aunt. I am 86 years old now, and so was about 11 years older than Peter. I remember that my Uncle Philly (we didn't call him Nip) worked for the town of Englewood taking care of the trees. We lived downstairs in a 2-story house in Fairview, New Jersey. We lived in one apartment and Peter and his family lived in the other apartment in the house. Uncle Philly and Aunt Ellen had the two boys and needed more space, so my mother and father spared them an additional room in our apartment.

I remember watching Peter embark out the door on his very first day of school. He had this cute, darndest walk and we all watched him go from the window, commenting on his confident swagger. He fit right in and liked school. Being a bit older than him, we were just so taken with his cuteness. He was such a good boy as a child.

The girls always liked Peter and he always had such a magnetic personality. He also had a knack for causing a bit of trouble but his cuteness made everyone love him. I used to babysit for Peter sometimes and I distinctly recall one memory when he climbed on top of the refrigerator and the entire refrigerator fell over. I was so worried that he had gotten hurt, but by some miracle he did not. His older brother, Philip, who was less prone to trouble, came running and I remember the shocked look on his face. We were all in shock that such a tiny human could have such a big impact.

***

<u>By Donnalee LaRose</u>

Spoken by Donnalee, written by Annmarie

My mother is Lena and my grandmother was Francie, which made me a cousin of Peter's. I am 66 years old now, so I was a young girl when I first knew cousin Peter. We lived in Massachusetts so I didn't have a lot of interaction with him, but I distinctly remember him coming to visit our family in Massachusetts when I was around ten years old. Peter was in his late teens, maybe 17 or 18, and I remember being awestruck with him. He was tall and handsome and had such an outgoing personality. We lived in a secluded area of Massachusetts and he was a "city" kid. I loved it when he came to visit (but I also remember being somewhat afraid to talk to him). For some reason, I remember that he came by himself, and I think it was by bus.[2]

My aunt Julia and her husband Carmen lived in Fairview, New Jersey. Julia had a slight frame, unlike most of the other siblings. I remember that she always had her hand around her stomach and she barely ate. Aunt Esther was much more dominant. My grandmother, Francie, was the wild one and it was well-known that she had a longtime boyfriend outside of her marriage. It fascinated me when I learned that my grandfather, Francie's husband, used to travel with his wife and her lover, Danny, all three of them together.

As an adult, I have a more recent memory of meeting Peter when my husband and I arrived in New Jersey for our family reunion in 2011. My late-

---

[2] Knowing my father, I am going to venture a theory that my grandparents had sent him to "the country" because they feared the very real alternative.

husband, Ernie, and Peter were meeting for the first time and somehow the conversation became about experiences they each had when they were younger. Peter told us a story I will never forget.

Peter and his friends were a confident, sly bunch. They were, as I interpreted it, a bunch of brats running around New York City, doing this and that to con people out of money. They may have even had small weapons, I don't know. They heard about a card game where they could potentially line their pockets, so Peter and his crew went to it. He told us that there were about 10 older men playing cards. They had no idea that, in Peter's words, they were about to "hold up the wrong game." All of the men were connected Italians (they came to learn) but Pete and his crew managed to take their money. After the game, a car followed Peter and his friends and an older guy got out and made them get in the car. He took the bunch to a bar in New York City, and another man, who they later came to know as the leader, came out and told Peter and his friends that it was "his money" that they took. Peter was around 17 at the time, and it was agreed that he would "work off" the money that he took at the game. He didn't say much more than that.

Peter was kind of an unforgettable and wonderful man.

***

My father reminded me many times over the years that I was the "first Gallione girl born in 52 years" in our immediate family, the last one being Francie. Perhaps this is why, when the aunts came to the party, I immediately gravitated toward Francie. We were the two youngest Gallione girls, even though there were 5 decades between us. This is also why I decided to resume use of the name "Gallione" when my father died. The name mattered to him, and it felt good to honor him in this way.

When I was old enough for my father to talk to me about such things, he mentioned Aunt Francie quite a lot. He knew that she and I felt a strong connection to one another, he thought we looked alike physically, and he surmised that thought the word "wild" fit both of us equally. (And…as these stories seem to be revealing, this trait was also commonplace in our family. So, we can blame that on genetics too.)

I remember asking my father why he never fully entered the world of the New York mafia, since it was clear that he had opportunities, like the one my cousin, Donnalee, recalled from her story. He was a bridge-distance away from New York City, spent most of his time there, and he was a proud Italian. He clearly wasn't concerned about breaking rules and had a penchant for violence anyway. In my mind, whenever I asked my dad about it, that "glamorous" lifestyle was so alluring that I couldn't imagine why he passed up any chance he was given.

His answer was fairly simple: in order to succeed in that world, one had to take orders, and my father didn't take direction from other people. One had to pay his dues and to patiently await his turn for his unwavering loyalty to be rewarded. That was just a whole lot of work and didn't interest my father. In any event, he garnered plenty of respect, fame, drugs, and romance on his own without having to be someone's underling. Hence, my father's story has very little to do with the North Jersey/New York mob.

Young Pete chose a different path than that, and also one much different than that which his his parents guided him towards. Because of them, my father's early life was filled with time spent with family, in service at the church, and in activities like Boy Scouts. They provided a nurturing and nourishing home for him and "did everything right", so to speak, but they were battling forces much larger than themselves when it came to my father and his addiction.

***

<u>*By Juliann Marrara Ardito*</u>

"My memories of my cousin Peter Gallione"

My name is Julieann Marrara Ardito and my memories of Pete will always be with me. I will try to bring them to life for you. Well, cousin Peter was 4 years older than me and actually was my second cousin. Peter's dad, Uncle Philly, was my Grandmother Julia's younger brother making my dad, Demetrio Marrara, Peter's first cousin. Big families make for big age differences.

I remember as a child going to visit Peter and his family, Uncle Philly, Aunt Ellen and cousin Philly, at their home in Englewood, New Jersey. I believe the house was on South Dean Street. After my dad parked the car, I remember walking down a dirt driveway between two buildings on either side. At the end of the driveway was a two-story square house. Peter and his family lived on the top floor. I remember walking up a wooden set of stairs and at the top was a long wooden porch with Cousins Peter and Philly waiting for company. I don't remember the inside because we just hung out on the wooden porch which seemed so high up. Whenever I am in the area, I always look at the spot where this house was. Like everything else, it is long gone.

On other occasions, Peter and his family would visit us in Fort Lee. My Grandmother, Julia, Pop Pop and Tommy lived upstairs from us so it was like a double visit. We all always played in the yard. As the years went on and we were all getting older, Peter told me he liked my neighbor, Barbara, who was the same age as Peter. He would come over with his family and always look over to our neighbor's yard. Nothing ever became of it, LOL.

Then one day when we went to visit Pete and his family, they weren't in Englewood but a big house on Tuxedo Square in Teaneck, New Jersey. We all hung out at the end of the driveway towards the back of the house. My dad always made me bring my accordion which, by the way, I was terrible at playing but I tried. Sometimes all the uncles and cousin Philly would be playing cards in the kitchen making a lot of noise.

I remember meeting Mary, your mom, for the first time and I was very impressed with teenagers. But sometimes cousin Peter's friends would show up and Peter would leave with them. This made Aunt Ellen, Peter's mom, very, very upset. As Peter was walking away, I can still see and hear Aunt Ellen standing in the driveway yelling "Peeeeeeter get back here", but he just kept on going. I wondered what was happening. Pete and I were talking about this not too long ago and I felt bad because, as we were talking about it, I could hear the regret in his voice.

We lost touch for quite some time, everyday life changes everything and everyone. When my Grandmother Julia passed away, probably in the early 80's, I remember Peter walking into Hunt's Funeral Home in Fort Lee. He didn't stay long but I remember him walking up to me and telling me if I ever needed anything or if anyone caused me trouble, to call him. I just knew he meant it.

More time had passed when Peter got in touch with me about a Gallione family reunion that he and Cousin Donnalee were working on for July 2010. It was so much fun to meet new cousins and family from Mexico. As you know, Peter was so, so happy. Then another much bigger reunion happened in 2019, which made Peter even happier. After speaking to him after that last reunion, I said to myself, it's a good thing you showed up, he was sad some people couldn't make it. We played phone tag here and there, especially on our birthdays. Mine is in June and his is in July. Last time I spoke to Peter was a few days after his last birthday. He was so excited about planning the next reunion, which was to be even bigger, and hopefully at the same park in Bergenfield if it could be arranged. He kept talking and I just kept saying, "Sounds great." He told me about his upcoming surgery. So I told him to keep me posted on how things were going.

I regret not knowing what was going on in Peter's life during his troubled years and lost so much time knowing each other. I regret never going to visit him in Florida after so many invites. I am grateful people saw his beautiful heart. I am also so grateful we reconnected and still had a warm place for each other in our hearts.

Rest In Peace, dear cousin. I will always remember that cute smiling face with those deep dimples. Oh, and my oldest son has dimples. You will always be in my prayers.

***

By Garry Bonnemere

As years pass and we get older, our time on Earth gets shorter. It's hard to think about and we push it to the back of our minds. But when a dear friend departs, we are jolted back to reality. Loss is a part of life that we can't avoid, but the best we can do is celebrate their life. Sometimes words of sympathy don't seem like enough, but know that these words come from the heart, especially when you've known the person as long as I've known Peter.

Growing up in New Jersey, Peter and I attended St. Cecilia's Grammar School, where we were altar boys. I was a year ahead of Peter at Teaneck High School and, to be honest, my recollections of those years are pretty cloudy. I do remember in those early days we would play touch football on weekends. Peter was pretty tough in those days and I was a lightweight, skinny kid. On this one particular autumn Saturday, we were playing and Peter laid me out... flat on my back! I knew then that I needed to find another sport to play (I ended up playing basketball). It's funny how certain memories stay with you over the years.

Although I lost contact with Peter after high school, Facebook brought us back in contact. It was great to have reconnected. I was not aware of Peter's problems, but I'm happy that he overcame them. It shows how strong of a person he was. We never discussed his situation but that wouldn't have changed our friendship.

I had hoped to have seen him in Florida in 2021. We had discussed getting together and I was so looking forward to it. Even though our visit won't happen, I can truly say that I'm glad I knew him and considered him a friend.

Rest In Peace, Peter, my friend.

24

Peter - first row, third from left; Garry - second row, farthest left

***

By Roni Malick

    Pete is front & center in the bottom row. Two of my brothers are in this & many other guys that I remember... I see Garry in that photo, too. I went to grade school with Pete & he was my first date (movies in Englewood) when we were in 8th grade. Absolutely, he was a gentleman. But... he put his arm around me, resting on my shoulders. By the end of the movie, I was in pain. He probably was also, LOL.

***

By Jim Gallione

Pete was my cousin, but he was more like a brother. I grew up in Northvale, and Pete was an integral part of my growing up. He had a special bond with my father, Alex ("Sonny"), and as a result he was always at family gatherings at our home. He so enjoyed being with family and that love of family (and friends) became the most important part of his life. Family was everything to Pete!

Through the years, he was always supportive of my involvement in sports — from juniors through college — and always trying to prove he was better than me (we were both very competitive). As I moved on to become a high school coach/athletic director, he continued to be supportive of my teams and involvement in athletics. He was one of my biggest fans!

Pete also was a caring and loving cousin to my brother, Jeff. He made a point of visiting him and talking and playing with him. Even from Florida, he made a point of keeping in touch with Jeff. He certainly demonstrated what family is all about in his caring relationship with Jeff.

Pete followed many paths in his life, but he became a positive and supportive influence for so many.

My wife, Sue, found a good friend to have conversations and debates with over the years. He was not just a friend but a source of strength and support to her even though there were miles between them. Our sons, Jimmy and Tommy, looked up to Pete and enjoyed any opportunity they got to spend with him.

There are many stories that I am sure can be shared about Pete. Our favorite is about Pete: the (self-proclaimed) "beach guy". One September after Labor Day, he wanted to use our condo in Wildwood Crest. Of course, this was not a problem and we gave him the key. Not even two days later, we got a call: "It's too cold! I need a sweater! I can't stay!". The temperature had dropped into the 60's and Pete was out of there. We had to laugh. Self-proclaimed beach guy, but only in Florida where it is always nice and HOT!

Pete was such an important member of my family from childhood on and he made a lasting impression on our "branch" of the Gallione family tree. We love and miss him.

***

<u>By Sal Messina</u>
Mary's cousin

As a young boy, Peter made a huge impression on me. He was a great athlete, which I always wanted to be, and he always had a smile on his face and an infectious giggle that made everyone want to be part of the fun. As I grew older, life happens and things happen. I remember when Peter came home. Ralph and I went to see Mary and Peter at their apartment in

Dumont. Man was he in shape! All buffed up from boxing. Again he made a huge impression on me. I was getting ready to play college basketball. I remember Peter asking me what my basketball goals were. Unhappy with my modest goals, Peter made me understand it was unacceptable to settle for less than my best and that I was capable of more. Again he made a huge impression on me. One I still live by today.

Rest In Peace, my friend.

***

My father experienced several significant turning points in his life, the earliest of which might have occurred on the day that he first saw my mother. He was young, but he was also romantic, even then, and so he recalled and told the story of that first encounter often. My father's family had just moved into the house in Teaneck, New Jersey and he was sitting on the porch steps. The year was 1959, and he was twelve years old. Some kids were playing stickball in the street and my father's attention was drawn to a young girl approximately his age who was tearing up the street yelling at the boys she was babysitting to get home. My mother's family had moved to New Jersey from 118th Street in Manhattan not long before, and she brought her city attitude with her.

According to my father, "he couldn't take his eyes off of her" and was instantly smitten. Those blue eyes, that dark skin, those legs and that moxy — which later earned her a nickname from him as his "roughneck from Harlem" — made for a dangerous and irresistible combination in my father's eyes. For the next 63 years, my mother and father shared a love that twisted and turned, bounded and waned, and eventually settled in to become a comfort for both of them at the end of his time on earth. It was both beautifully real and tragically painful throughout the years, but what true love isn't?

***

By Mary Gallione

Peter's First Wife and Annmarie's Mother
Written by Eve Jensen

I first encountered Peter in the spring of 1959, when I was twelve years old. I had been babysitting in Teaneck, and I was running up Tuxedo Square screaming at my charges. Peter had moved in recently, and that day he was sitting on his porch as I came howling up the street. We didn't officially meet then, but he told me years later that was the moment I caught his eye. He met my younger brother, Charles, through Boy Scouts, and that's how we actually came to know each other. He used to come over and play stickball in the street with Charles and our other cousins and friends.

I always knew he was sweet on me, but I didn't fall in love with him right away. Even though it took me some time to reciprocate his feelings, he was always willing to do things for me and he was very protective of me. I think we were still 12 years old when we started dating. We often hung out at Cole's, the shoppe where I used to work, and eventually we would go to drive-in movies and diners.

We were both stubborn, and fought quite a bit. I remember one fight we had when I was sixteen or seventeen. I don't remember what the fight itself was about, but I remember being so angry that I chopped all my hair off later that night. As soon as I did, I panicked. I knew he was going to freak out when he saw me. My friends and I went to a pizza place, and when we saw him coming, we all ran into the bathroom and hid. We stayed there until my best friend Gloria told us the coast was clear.

As soon as I exited the bathroom, though, he came out from where he was hiding across the street. I took off out of the restaurant and he chased me down the block. I turned into an alley and a cat was sitting right there, staring at me. I screamed, turned around, and ran right back into him. I remember him grabbing my arms and saying, "You're afraid of the cat, but not me?" It was a stupid question, really. Cats are evil. And besides, I always felt safe when I was with him.

Everyone who knew Peter during this time knew that he was a tough guy. He was always getting into trouble for fighting or drugs or anything else he could possibly get into trouble for. And I had to be there for all of it. I hated his friends, because they were always getting him mixed up in fights. The night of my senior prom, he was supposed to drive Gloria and I to an afterparty, but first he had to go to a fight in Fort Lee. I drove around for hours that night in my prom dress and heels, not sure if he was actually at the fight or if he was cheating on me.

We were engaged multiple times, once on the side of the highway, before we actually made it down the aisle. It was a beautiful wedding. But we were only married for about two years before Peter started doing drugs again. I told him to leave. I didn't realize how much I truly loved him until I had. Despite our split, however, he still remained firmly a part of my family. He regularly played cards with my mother, which they both enjoyed immensely. Not to mention, I was pregnant.

We were already divorced when Annmarie was born, but that never stopped him from being present and involved throughout the pregnancy, during the birth, and further on into her childhood. He loved her more than anything. When she was two years old, however, he got sentenced to prison for aggravated assault. He was sentenced on November 30, 1973. He put the Christmas tree up for us before he went away so that he could celebrate the holiday with us that year.

When Peter went away, he first went to Trenton State Prison, which was a maximum-security jail. I visited him there with his mother and brother but I refused to bring the baby there. I can still hear the metal doors slamming in my mind.

He was eventually transferred to a medium security prison in Leesburg, where I agreed to bring Annmarie, then finally to minimum security. There, he was allowed to come home on weekend furloughs. I would leave Bergenfield at three in the morning to pick him up by 6:30 on Fridays, and he would drive us back home. He would spend the weekend up north until we had to drive him back again on Sunday; he still enjoyed playing poker with my Mom whenever he was home.

By the time he was released, we didn't talk as often, though Annmarie was always able to go see him down south and he was always invited to her events and came as much as he could. Their love for one another grew and grew. As Annmarie grew and eventually gave us grandkids, we remained family always. He would even stay with me any time he came up to New Jersey from Florida. I am proud of him for the father and grandfather he was, and for turning his life around, though I worried every day that he would go back to doing drugs. I asked him about this once, about if he or anyone else worried the same. He told me, "you worry because you're the only one who really knows me."

I think people often want to hear that we had a perfect, beautiful love story. I often want to give them that. But our relationship wasn't perfect. We were both stubborn and headstrong. We fought often. He cheated often. We broke up often. But we loved each other strongly, fiercely, and eternally. I used to believe that once you were lovers with someone, you could never be friends. But Peter was the love of my life, and my closest friend in the end.

***

I have no recollection of my parents living together. By the time 1971 rolled around, my father was pretty comfortably niched in the addiction abyss. The pictures of him during that time period are disturbing and I am glad that he will be remembered differently by most people. He worried, often out loud and sometimes in his letters, that he had genetically predisposed me to addiction and this concern was one of his ways of attempting to discourage me from using hard drugs.

My understanding is that my parents, having married on April 27, 1969, were already well on their way to divorce when I was conceived in mid-1970.

This fact made for interesting conversation since their separation allowed my mother to pinpoint the time of conception. I remember the conversation with my mother well: it was awkward (but she answered my questions), romantic (in a literary way), and, mostly, it caused me to panic. Once I put it all together and realized that I was conceived at the very end of my parents' time together, my life kind of passed before my eyes. I think I even exclaimed, "I almost wasn't born!!" And now, 50 years later, that acknowledgment still creates immense gratitude in me for the life that I have been given. My parents were together from the tender age of 12, their marriage lasted for a hot minute, and their friendship and parenting partnership endured for his entire lifetime.

***

By Gloria Riccitelli
Mary's best friend and Annmarie's godmother

I first met Pete when I was 15 years old. I was best friends with Mary. We always had great times together. I remember all the block dances we would go to, we all loved dancing. All the times just riding around. There were many times Mary and myself would be running through Teaneck because we heard Pete and his friends were going to be in a confrontation with guys from another town.

Pete was really a great guy. Although he had another side of him when it came to Mary seeing someone else. His jealousy really showed.

Pete's love for Mary was always obvious. Finally, in 1969 they were married. The best was yet to come. The birth of their beautiful daughter Annmarie. Their family was complete. She was their life.

Even though the marriage didn't last, Annmarie always came first. Later, Pete would be incarcerated. Mary would never say anything bad to Annmarie about her dad. Pete went to college while in prison and received a degree. Pete went on to help others take the right path in life as he did.

Pete and Mary went on to see Annmarie turn into a beautiful young woman. She went on to graduate law school, become an exceptional lawyer, get married and have two beautiful children, Evie and Nathaniel. All three became Mary and Pete's world. They couldn't be more proud of them.

Pete and Mary would always be there for each other, no matter what. I didn't stay in touch with Pete, but Mary would always keep me up to date. I would see Pete at many functions. In all the years I knew Pete, we never had a fight, and I'm thankful for that.

The things I'll miss about Pete are his contagious smile and his beautiful dimples. Till we all meet again, Rest in Peace. You are now home with Mom, Dad and Philip.

Love, Gloria

***

There can be little doubt in anyone's mind that my father was a "ladies' man", nor was it ever any secret that he utilized his cuteness to his advantage. He had a youthfulness about him, even late in life, and relished his continued good looks. My father honestly acknowledged that he was insecure about a lot of things when he was young and that those insecurities led him to his addiction and his violent lifestyle. His looks were not usually one of those insecurities.

*** *** ***

By Suzanne Genovese

I had not seen or been in touch with your dad since high school — well, maybe a few times at Rocklins parking lot after graduation — until recently on Facebook. But I have always thought about him as our yearbook stated: "Duke of the School". He walked and talked with attitude and control. Which is why it's not surprising to me that he overcame addiction and all that goes with it. I did hear early on that he had his struggles, but really... who could stay mad at those dimples? I will miss his postings on Facebook. There is always a special place in your heart for high school friends.

Peter Gallione
Duke of the School.

***

The next major turning point in my father's life was the onset of his drug addiction, first heroin and then, later, cocaine. During his adolescence and his twenties, my father became largely unrecognizable to those who knew him as that sweet, dark-complected boy with a smile and dimples that could drop you to your knees. He was in and out of juvenile detention and ran away from home for stretches at a time. He was beyond the control of his parents and most other authority figures.

My father's eventual rehabilitation enabled him to accept and to share with us the reasons why he chose an uncharacteristic life filled with drugs and violence, despite being raised in a thoroughly loving home. It is complex, of course, but the short of it is that my father harbored many insecurities about himself. Self-love did not come easy to him, but fighting did. He battled a plethora of internal demons and at some point figured out that he could earn the "respect" of people around him simply by taking it. He possessed significant physical prowess, both in life and in love, and learned how to use it to his advantage. He played semi-pro football, was a great baseball player, and messed around here and there in the boxing ring. Unfortunately, the drugs made him feel even more invincible and less concerned about the rules, and so his prowess turned to violence.

At this point in his explanation about "*why?*", my father was always sure to state that he did not, at any point, target innocents. He wasn't the bully; he was the kid that "*knocked out*" the bully. He didn't rob people who didn't deserve to be robbed, i.e. he only took money and drugs from other dealers. He would never-ever-ever-ever strike a woman. And if he learned that you did — well, you surely created a difficult situation for yourself in that event. He liked to think of himself as a "*good, bad guy.*"

***

By Buzzy Schioli

Spoken by Buzzy, Written by Annmarie

I knew right then, at the sound of his chuckle on the other end of the phone, that there would be some things that he would take to his own grave.

"You are the only source of information that I have for some of these events," I told him.

"Yes, and that is the way it will stay," he responded convincingly.

My father's relationship with Buzzy Schioli began in 1961. It was a chosen brotherhood that took different paths, but lasted until the very end. I made the mistake of calling Buzzy from my father's phone on the day that he died. I wasn't thinking and I just pulled up his name and hit call. I realized after I tried (and failed) to speak, that Buzzy expected it to be my father's voice on the other end. Getting the words out to tell him that dad died was arduous and ugly, painful and nauseating. It was, to put it simply, excruciatingly emotional.

Buzzy's reaction to hearing that my father had passed is something that will bring tears to my eyes each and every time I think about it, and certainly as I try to express it now. It was the sound of anger and pain and love and 60 years-worth of kinship all wrapped up and shouted to the universe over and over. I heard the word "Motherfucker!!" a lot, and I now realize that he was yelling at my father for leaving him. It went on for a while, cursing and denying and then apologizing and then more cursing and crying and disbelief. During that time, as my mom and I listened to him and cried our own tears, I realized that Buzzy was the last one of my father's "gang" to remain alive. Buzzy was the last man standing. And he was pissed about it.

When I was young and my father told me about The Magnificent Seven (yes, you read that right and no, not the movie), it was pretty fascinating. If only I had written those stories down, I could share more now but my father's storytelling gave the history so much flavor that my writing could not do it justice. Buzzy, as I said, would only share so much.

The Magnificent Seven, in addition to being a western from 1960, was the self-proclaimed group that my father ran with in his youth: him, Buzzy, John A., Paul R. (from east Harlem), Danny F., Eddie W., Matt M. and Jack B.[3] Here is Buzzy's first-hand account:

We were a bunch of fighters who grew to have respect for one another. It was such a nice suburban town and we were a bunch of Italian bad boys. Even the black kids didn't mess with us.

We started making money by robbing drug dealers but we didn't care because we were the tough guys. I would never take the drugs, just the money. We always had lots of girls around us. Everyone was afraid of us and we had a reputation. The cops were glad that

---

[3] Try telling them to their face that they added up to 8 and not 7 and see where it landed you.

we kept bad news from other towns out, so we got away with a lot.

If you fought one of us then you fought all of us. Some guys from Brooklyn came over and jumped out on Cedar Lane one time. Every guy your father hit was knocked out. Every time. Pete had a way of getting all of his weight behind his punch. He had a knack for punching that I really appreciated – I trained hard but he had a natural gift.

Pete was vicious at times – you didn't just hit someone, you hurt them. He was both a vicious hoodlum and a nice guy.

I wanted to fight as a boxer so I didn't do drugs. I trained at Gleason's in New York. Pete was my biggest fan and always came to watch me. He thought I was going to be the champion of the world.

Pete started doing heavier drugs and I wasn't into that. He got a bit wild and started to get into some real bad stuff. We were living together in a house in Englewood Cliffs. I had a girl and Pete had a girl. He got pinched a bunch of times.

One thing that I will discuss is the tattoo that each of the crew had. Paul came up with the idea and Pete did my tattoo in 1964. We called it "the crosses" and it came from a Mexican gang or something.

We had a special thing, me and Pete. I give him a lot of credit for turning his life around. And we were just getting to be close again. That guy was very special.

***

By Judi Urdang Gubenko

Writing this is very hard for me. I loved Peter so much as a friend, a person and how he turned his life around. But I don't know how many people know how this happened!

Pete left Teaneck High I think in his senior year, I'm really not sure. But he came back to clean out his locker and ran into Mr. Charlie Gunner. Mr. Gunner was the Vice Principal of THS and had a heart-to-heart talk with Pete, telling him how important it was to finish high school and HAVE A DIPLOMA. The rest is history because when Pete went to "Camp" he was able to attend Glassboro State. He graduated, got a degree and ended up with a pension!! All because of Charlie Gunner.

How did I meet the famous bad boy Pete Gallione? I was I think around 14/15 years old at a dance at Ben Franklin Junior High during the summer. He asked me to dance!!! I was so nervous because HE WAS PETE GALLIONE. Great dancer, and I liked those dimples and eyes instantly! I said to myself: he's so sweet what is everyone talking about?! The next dance was a slow one and this really cute guy tapped Pete on his shoulder and asked if he could cut in! Holy Shit, it was Buzzy, I was dancing with Buzzy, and from then on I was Buzzy's girl!!

The rumble on Cedar Lane was very memorable! We were all standing around but the guys knew *something was going to happen and happen fast! Some bad guys from the Bronx or Washington Heights were coming. Next, Matt M is thrown through the Cedar Lane Pizza window!!! All of a sudden I'm picked up by my waist and carried away! I'm yelling, "Peter you're hurting me and why are you doing this!" He throws me over his shoulder like he's a fireman! Ok, not the best position to be in but he says, "You are Buzzy's girl and he doesn't want you here!" He literally drops me in a corvette with Richie M! Long story short we all end up at my house. That was a safe zone.*

Judi learns to drive a stick shift. I just turned 16 and the dynamite duo Pete, Judi and Buzzy were going to Washington Heights to drink! We are going up Cedar Lane, Pete's in his car, I'm with Buzzy. Pete slams on his brakes right before the bridge, jumps out, opens passenger door and tells ME TO DRIVE!! I said we have 2 problems. 1- I don't have a license and Pete said he didn't either (great) 2- I don't know how to drive a stick! No problem. In 30 seconds I learned and off we went. I left his car at my house and the 3 of us drove to NYC.

And the amazing thing is I never got into trouble with my parents. They loved Peter and my house was the hangout! Sometimes on weekdays there would be at least 10 Corvettes, 57 Chevy's! My parents were great because they knew where their daughter was!

My best friend Beryl and I went to Florida for our spring break. We were at some hotel listening to a great band. The drummer was cute and Beryl was talking to the guitar player. Then the guitar players girlfriend shows up and starts giving Beryl a hard time! Not on my watch. Next she punches me and I gave her an upper right hand, to the chin (thanks Pete for that lesson) and we ran like hell!! We walk outside the hotel and who is leaning against their car? Pete and Buzzy!!! What the fuck!! I have ice on my lip and a Pete says "who threw the 1st punch?" I replied she did because YOU TAUGHT ME WELL!!!

I lost touch with Pete but ran into him in Teaneck in the 70s. We exchanged phone numbers and kept in touch. Then he was gone! Just like that, I had no idea where, when or how or what happened to the bad boy who was my protector. Peter was always there for me. We talked for hours on the phone, then he was gone.

Thank you Facebook! We reconnected and it was like we never lost touch. He filled me in on "Camp", about his beautiful daughter Annmarie and his grandchildren. Peter was living in Pompano Beach Florida and I'm in Delray Beach. I said Roadtrip!!

Peter and I spoke on the phone very often. Sometimes for over an hour. He loved to reminisce about the good old days. After John A died he said that he and Buzzy were the only 2 left of the group! He was sad, but he starts to tell me about Jack B's funeral. I said what did you do? He said he didn't think Jack was dead! What are you talking about? So all the guys go the funeral home and are standing around the casket and Peter and Buzzy try to lift the lid to make sure Jack was in there! But it was sealed!! They believe that he was in some kind of witness protection program! Ok, you are crazy!

But it's amazing what we talked about! Also never call Peter at 4:00 because he took a nap with his fan! Loved his fan.

He told me he wanted to do plantings in his backyard around his pool. I said, "who am I talking to?" he said, "I know, but what about shrimp plants?" You have lost your mind but I'll be down Tuesday.

I fell in love with his home. It had Peter Gallione written all over it and the backyard definitely needed work! Roadtrip to the nursery on Dixie Highway. But across the street was the Goodyear Blimp! It is Huge! I couldn't stop staring at it and Peter kept saying, "Focus on plants!" He grabs my hand and says, "Come on Sis we got work to do!!"

Peter spent all the Jewish holidays with us. He loved my brisket. And came to our granddaughters Sophia's birthdays. He is family.

If I had a problem or issue I called my brother. He was always there for me, always! Stupid things like getting over the water on the 6th hole. I just couldn't do it!! I'd call from the car and he would say well, "did you?" No, and he would have words of encouragement "YOU WILL." The week after Peter died, I GOT OVER THE FUCKEN' WATER!! Because my Big Brother was watching!

I miss him so very much and I know so many others do too. He was my mentor, my psychologist, my Rabbi and everything a big brother is supposed to be!

Annmarie I can keep going and going but one more thing. When Charlie Gunner died Peter flew up for his funeral and gave a eulogy and told his story how Charlie Gunner saved his life!

Thank you for letting me share a small part of my crazy experiences with Peter. I will not remove him from my house phone or cell, because I want him with me always.

Love hugs and kisses, Judi Urdang Gubenko

***

PART TWO
THE MIDDLE YEARS

The reason that my father disappeared, as Judi recalled, is that on August 9, 1973, he hit a defining moment in his era of criminal escapades and drug abuse.

At this most significant turning point of his life, my father and two of his associates initiated and attempted to conduct a drug con that went wrong. For context, one of the ways that my father and his friends earned their living in those days was by, as he put it, *"sticking up drug dealers"*. They realized that they could generate even more income simply taking money from dealers by force after luring them into a seemingly-legitimate deal rather than by going through the trouble of actually selling them drugs, which they also wanted for themselves.

For some reason that is beyond me, the plan worked more than once. Thus my father was able to not only feed his habit with the drugs that he got his hands on, but he could then further feed that habit by stealing money from dealers looking to purchase large quantities that he promised but never delivered. From time to time, rather than complete the drug transaction, my father and his guys would simply rob the others of the purchase money… and keep the drugs. The reason why the heist failed on that Thursday night in August, however, is that, unbeknownst to them, their targets were undercover members of New Jersey State Police and the Hackensack and Paramus Narcotics Detective Units.

Since he eventually pleaded guilty to several of the offenses with which he was charged as a result of the events of August 9, it is fair to let the gravamen, or the "essence", of the Indictment filed in the matter of *State of New Jersey vs. Peter Gallione, et al.* tell part of the story[4]:

The Grand Jurors of the State of New Jersey, for the County of Bergen, upon their oaths present that PETER GALLIONE, [Co-Defendant 1] and [Co-Defendant 2], on or about the 9th day of August, 1973, in the City of Hackensack in the County of Bergen aforesaid, and within the jurisdiction of this Court, did unlawfully and feloniously make an assault upon DETECTIVE HEINZ ASMUSS and ANDRE SESTIC, with the intent then and there to steal, take and carry away the property, goods, money and chattels of the said DETECTIVE HEINZ ASMUSS and ANDRE SESTIC feloniously, forcibly and violently against their will, and by putting them in fear...

SECOND COUNT
[...] did unlawfully, by speech, while holding a .32 caliber revolver, threaten feloniously to take and procure the taking of

---

[4] Transcribed from official Indictment.

the life of DETECTIVE HEINZ ASMUSS and ANDRE SESTIC...

THIRD COUNT

[...] the said PETER GALLIONE. . .unlawfully carried a certain firearm, to wit, a .32 caliber revolver, Titanic, Serial No. [omitted], concealed on and about his clothes and person without first having obtained the requisite permit to carry the same...

[FOURTH AND FIFTH COUNTS OF CO-DEFENDANTS OMITTED]

SIXTH COUNT

[...] willfully and unlawfully obstructed, opposed, and hindered JAMES SCOTT and RICHARD MEDASKA, of the Hackensack Police Department, and HEINZ ASMUSS, New Jersey State Police, in the lawful execution of their duties by resisting arrest by willfully and unlawfully striking the said Policemen...

SEVENTH COUNT

[...] did commit the crime of conspiracy in that then and there they did unlawfully conspired together with intent to distribute a controlled dangerous substance to wit: MARIJUANA...

EIGHTH COUNT

[...] did commit the crime of conspiracy in that then and there they unlawfully conspired together to obtain money from DETECTIVE ASMUSS by false pretenses, to wit, by knowingly, fraudulently and falsely pretending to the said DETECTIVE ASMUSS that in exchange for $5,000.00 the said PETER GALLIONE, [Co-Defendant 1] and [Co-Defendant 2], were to give to DETECTIVE ASMUSS a suitcase which contained $5,000.00, worth of Marijuana, when in truth and fact said suitcase contained nothing of value.

OVERT ACTS

And that in execution of the aforesaid conspiracy and to effect the object thereof the overt acts following were done:

1.   Peter Gallione and [Co-Defendant 1] were hiding on the fifth floor of the Carlysle Apartments located at 380 Prospect Avenue, Hackensack.

2.   [Co-Defendant 2] went to the car of Detective Asmuss and there discussed a narcotic transaction; counting out $5,000.00 given to him by Detective Asmuss.

3.   After having counted the $5,000.00, Detective Asmuss and [Co-Defendant 2] and Andre Sestic went to the fifth floor of the said apartment building, for the purpose of acquiring narcotics.

4.   After arriving at apartment 5A of said apartment building, Peter Gallione and [Co-Defendant 1] emerged from a hiding place in the hallway. Peter Gallione placed a gun to the head of Detective Asmuss and Andre Sestic.

**5.   In exchange for the aforesaid
$5,000.00, the said Peter Gallione, [Co-
Defendant 1] and [Co-Defendant 2] were to
give to Detective Asmus a suitcase which
contained $5,000.00 worth of Marijuana,
when in truth and fact, said suitcase
contained nothing of value...**

In layperson's terms, my father and his two co-conspirators had been the target of an undercover operation for several weeks and had been suspected of selling large quantities of hard drugs from a 5th floor apartment at the Carlyle Apartments in Hackensack, New Jersey. The undercover agents arranged to make a $5,000.00 purchase of marijuana from them and, instead, became the victims of an attempted armed robbery. As my dad used to tell it, the con artists got conned and then all hell broke loose. An officer got hurt, but lived — thank goodness — and my father and his accomplices were eventually arrested with the help of several backup members of the narcotics teams. Bail for each of them was set at $100,000.00, a sizable sum at any time and certainly in 1973.

A newspaper article published the next day, August 10, 1973, was titled "Undercover narcotics agent faces death — lives". The article reported that "about 10 men from the Hackensack, Paramus and the state police narcotics divisions had surrounded the area", expecting a routine drug sale that would lead to an arrest for distribution. Hackensack Police Chief Anthony Iurato was quoted as saying that the backup officers "had to bust in the door to prevent a murder." The way my father explained it, a shot was fired through the apartment door from the hallway and he shot back, believing that he and his associates were about to become the victims of a robbery, themselves. The incident was described by Chief Iurato as a "brief but violent fight." It may have been that the lock was shot by the officers on the outside of the door to open it and my father shot back in response. It is unclear why the weapon firings are not mentioned in the Indictment, but one possibility is that the initial discharge by the police officer would have, if unauthorized, complicated the State's case against my father.

At some point after he learned that the purported dealers were actually law enforcement, my father managed to get himself to the balcony of the apartment and to disarm himself of his weapon. A supplemental report prepared by an officer from the Hackensack Police Department states that the .32 pistol was found *"lying in the weeds northside of the building"* after officers were dispatched to find it *"at daybreak"* on August 10, 1973. The suitcase that was supposed to contain the drugs, but which actually contained newspapers and books, was also thrown out of a window. Only a "minute quantity" of drugs were actually found in the apartment. Interestingly, the article also reported that all three men possessed airplane tickets, "possibly for escape purposes".

When my father got far enough away from the night of the incident to make light of it, he would say that he was extremely thankful for 3 things that happened that night: 1) that he was arrested; 2) that a police officer had not gotten killed; and 3) that he also didn't shoot a *"little old lady"* who may have been walking by when he hurled his gun as far as he possibly could from that 5th floor balcony in the hope that it would never be found.

On October 24, 1973, he pleaded guilty to the first and second counts of the Indictment and was thus convicted of aggravated assault and threat to kill. On November 30, 1973, my father was sentenced by the New Jersey Superior Court to 5 to 7 years confinement in New Jersey State Prison on the first count and 3 to 5 years on the second count, the latter to run concurrent with the former. The remaining counts were dismissed.

Another article that featured my father, this one published in the Courier Post newspaper on December 19, 1993, twenty years after the night of his final crime, quotes him explaining what happened from his perspective: "'I was ripped,' said Gallione, 'And when you're that ripped, you don't care about anything.'"

Former addict: 'Face it . . . our laws are not working'

Later in his life, long after his sentence was served, my father would credit this arrest, and the incarceration and rehabilitation that followed, to saving his own life. There is zero question that he was on an extremely destructive path and he recognized he was fortunate that law enforcement got him before cocaine and heroin did.

He was committed first to Trenton State Prison, a rough place, even for a seemingly hard guy like my father. In the very first letter from jail[5] that we have from him, dated December 14, 1973, two weeks after the start of his imprisonment, my father mused: "*Boy, I'm in some mess. I really did it this time.*" He also gave my mother this assurance, which it turns out he upheld for the remainder of his life:

> *I don't know what the future holds, but I promise one thing, when I get out, I'll try to be a better person, especially a better father... I miss you and the baby. I was thinking of asking you to bring her down here, but I don't think I could take it. She got on the phone the other day when I called my mother and I started to cry. Baby I wonder where I went wrong. It was probably a long time ago.*

---

[5] Anything that is shared here is either directly from my father's letters to me or is shared with my mother's permission.

In another early letter, he told my mother about a horrible experience he had while at Trenton State, and also shared his feelings about fatherhood:

You say I'm getting to be a good father, well I'm trying I really am. I do love her very much but really can't do much about it now. I have to wait until I get out to really act like her father. A tragedy happen[ed] here this morning. They locked a 19 year old boy up in solitary confinement for doing something wrong and somehow during the night a hot steam pipe broke in his cell and he was screaming for his life and the guards didn't even listen to him. They found him dead early this morning" [12/28/73].

During his early time in prison, my father did a lot of thinking, and his letters are a treasure trove of those thoughts, both good and bad. Those were extremely rough days for him. I am sure that having to write messages like, *"Daddy... wishes he could be there with you, but promises that once he gets home he will never miss another Christmas with you"* helped my father to stay committed to his recovery, which was a long and arduous road [12/26/73]. My mother, knowing what she knew of my father's past, pleaded with him not to make me promises that he would not keep. But my father kept making promises to me, letter after letter, and we know now that he found the wherewithal to keep those promises until the day that he died.

Even though they were divorced, my parents' love for one another persisted and they attempted to mend their relationship during his incarceration. My mother provided a connection to me and a lifeline to the outside world that he needed to survive inside. She also handled many of his affairs, along with my grandmother, and made sure that he was always stocked with stamps so that he could keep getting his letters out. She reluctantly agreed to visit him during his time at Trenton State, but was firm about the fact that two-and-a-half year old me would never step foot inside of it. My father and I, therefore, did not see one another for several months, until he was transferred to Leesburg State Prison, a medium security institution, even farther from our home, in the spring of 1974.

Reading his letters back then must have been as wretched for my mother as they were for me when I got older. Many, many tears were shed reading the inner workings of my father's mind in those days — the remorse, the fear and the anguish of it all, the desperation and the love. It is said that there is beauty in the struggle, and this is what I repeatedly tried to remind myself as I re-read his letters as an adult and absorbed the despair that he experienced at that time in his life.

For my father, the beauty was in finding a life's purpose through his incarceration. He used his time in confinement to better himself, to become a better father, to further his education, to understand his addiction, and to counsel others through their own. Anyone who knew him when he went in, and still knew him when he came out, would surely reach unanimous agreement that his transformation was remarkable.

The regular correspondence between my parents for those three years, and our many visits with him, enabled my father to show my mother that he could, indeed, be a good father. My father's letters always encouraged me to *"be good for Mommy"* and he regularly chastised me when her last one to him had reported some trouble that I caused. She usually blamed him for whatever it was, and he usually accepted fault. Throughout my childhood, that pattern continued, with my father getting "the blame", mostly in jest, whenever I was difficult. Even then, my parents had worked out a somewhat effective parenting dynamic and an understanding that, if I was disobedient, it was because of his genetics, not hers.

In the initial months, the first page of his letters would be to me, written thoroughly from top to bottom and side to side, since paper was a limited resource in prison. They usually began *"Hi, Baby"* and were filled with sweet sentiments and apologies (which he clearly meant). He regularly asked me about my mom's family, many of whom he also corresponded with, and about his dog, Hondo, that he left in the care of close friends of ours and who he missed about as much as he missed me. He always inquired about my dance recitals and whatever else I was into at the time and routinely bestowed some nugget of wisdom upon me which, now, as a parent, I deeply recognize the value of. He often stressed the value of school and friendships and encouraged me to trust the doctors who were trying to make my troublesome ears feel better.

My father's voice comes through very clearly in his writing and he often joked with me, asking things like *"What's this about the high dive. You can't go off that until daddy is around. Mommy's not a great swimmer, you know? How is she? Fine I hope. Give her a kiss for me, okay?"* [4/26/74]. Sometimes, he sent a message to my mother through his letters to me, e.g. *"Tell Mommy her skirts are too short and she should wear them longer, because she doesn't listen to Daddy anymore"* [12/28/73]. Always, he reminded us that I possessed *"not only [his] good looks, but also [his] intelligence and good sense of humor"* [12/31/73].

He joked with my mom, too, especially when it came to the length of her letters. *"You say your letters are long, its really your paper is too short and not wide enough"* [1/9/74]. Back then, my father forgot that he had a lot more time on his hands than my mother did, being that she was working full-time and raising a little girl on her own. As I said, there are actually two heroes in this story.

My mother started me roller skating very young and so my father wrote me things like *"be careful when you go out skating and always hold onto Mommy's hand"* [1/9/74], while in his corresponding letter sent for her eyes only, he wrote "*Are you sure she won't get hurt on those skates, she's still a little young isn't she?*" I was too young to read them myself but my mother read each of my letters to me, sometimes several times. And she regularly wrote back to him on my behalf.

At the ages of two and a half through five and a half, I grew increasingly better at understanding and communicating back to my father. My mother's letters to him from me told him of my accomplishments and challenges and also told him things that she knew would aggravate him, because his responses were usually entertaining. We don't have most of her letters but we do have copies of a few. With her permission, here is the letter that "we" wrote on March 6, 1974, shortly before I turned 3 years old, which also illustrates my mother's sense of humor:

> *Dear Daddy,*
>
> *Hello! How are you? I am fine. Right now I am at the laundromat with mommy. We received your letter today and I told mommy we had to write to daddy. So here it goes. I play at Grandma's house all day. When it's nice out, I play outside & I ride my bike. Mommy said she will take me roller skating when she's not working. I like to talk to you on the phone. Did you ask your boss if you can come home & fix my hairdryer? Do I have to wait till I get big like Aunt Nancy for your boss to let you come home? Know what, mommy says when I get bigger I can*

come to where you work. And pretty soon my birthday is coming and I'll be bigger. For my birthday, I told mommy I want to go to the rides, a candy factory, Dinah-mite & the Beach House & to go see daddy. But mommy says I'm too small for the beach house, and daddy is getting the candy factory, & she will take me & my cousin Edward & my Aunt Nancy to the rides & we'll see about my coming to where you work. Do you want to see me? Mommy says if I don't stop bugging her about coming to see you she won't take me at all. I'm mad at her. My ears pierced don't hurt me anymore. Daddy I'm going to play now. I'll write again. I love you & I hope God keeps you safe & lets you come home soon.

Love & kisses oxox
Your little angel,
Annmarie

On the back of each of his letters to me, my father always began his letter to my mother and that correspondence continued for several more pages, top to bottom and front to back, leaving virtually no blank space unless it was lockup or it was time for him to go to school or work. Several of them, he wrote while sneaking in the bathroom stall late at night because it was the only place where he had access to light. Those early communications from my father (which respond to those from my mother) are deep and complex and personal. Reading them showed me a side to both of my parents that was vividly painful and beautiful. Their love story is a story for another day, if my mother wishes for it to be shared.

Sometimes, my father wrote to me about the importance of school, especially as I got older and he got deeper into his own education through the prison program. He wrote to my mother on June 9, 1975, just after I turned four years old, and asked her if she was considering enrolling me in Kindergarten in the fall. According to my father, some people started kids that early. Education, not just his own, but as a matter of public health, became *extremely* important to my father and he was fortunate to be able to attend college simultaneously while serving his time. In January of 1975, after I had dropped out of several different nursery schools, my father wrote to my mother about my early aversion to school and his concern in this regard. *"We've got to come up with some kind of con to reverse her feelings"* [1/13/75]. Apparently, that "con" was successful, because I eventually grew to love school and learning, much like my father during that time period.

Gallione, Peter

A resident at Leesburg State
Prison, Leesburg, N. J.
609-785-0040
Is Employed at:

State College Student

Glassboro, N.J.
on **WORK RELEASE** as authorized by
Chapter 22, Public Laws of 1969.

Asst. Superintendent   Date

Idle time was a bad thing for my father in jail,
and so he wrote often and extensively. The letters show
a side to him that probably most have never seen. In the
early days, his mind was full of self-defeat, counting
days and hours and worrying about getting out. We
know now that, in those first few months, my father
was just trying to play a game to beat the system. He
was used to conning people and so he joined the drug
program and enrolled in school because he thought that
was his surest way out as fast as possible. He wasn't so
much interested in getting well as he was in getting out.

He talked a lot about staying out of trouble while
inside so that he could maximize his chance of earning
parole at his first hearing in March of 1975. In the
beginning, and up to that first parole hearing, my
father's mind was frequently consumed with being
released, as I imagine most prisoner's minds are. Even
though he assured my mother that he wasn't going to

run once he had the opportunity, it had to be extremely nerve-wracking for her to read "*This time is murdering me baby*" and to worry about what my father might do if he broke bad again.

When he was transferred to the minimum security institution at Leesburg, known as "The Farm", my mother expressed her concern that he would run away and my father wrote this to her on October 26, 1974:

Are you really concerned about me up and leaving? Don't be. I promise I'll stay here until they allow me to go home. I can't be really free unless they let me and I've already given them this much. I won't ever jeopardize my chances for this coming March.

He repeatedly talked about how he had to figure out a way not to ever return to that place. Thus, my father dove headfirst into the Alpha-Meta drug program, which gave him a ticket out of Trenton and into Leesburg, and eventually to "The Farm", where the privileges were much more extensive, mostly because of the possibility of furlough release.

The living conditions are horrible and dirty. No privacy and it is boring as hell. I'm in Phase II of the drug program and my institutional job is Co-Ordinator of the program. So at least I don't have to milk cows or work with the pigs or anything like that. The only good thing about being out here is that I am eligible for my furloughs. If there was no such thing as furloughs, everyone would be killing each other to get back inside of the prison. I hate it, but I want to be home with you and the baby for Christmas [10/20/74].

By August of 1974, less than a year into his sentence, he had obtained a job on staff of the drug program. In September of 1974, he wrote to us and told us that he wanted to show us a brochure that he made for it but he didn't have enough stamps for it so he would show us if my mother told him ahead of the next time she planned to visit. During these months, when the program started to hit my father differently, and he realized that he wasn't just doing it for show, he would write things like *"my future is cloudy and mysterious...but it is also wide open"*. [9/27/74]. He talked a lot about *"helping the youth"* and making sure that nothing was going to be the same when he came out. Still, you could sense the hope within my father's heart: *"I know there is a place for me somewhere on this earth, yet I can't seem to find it"* [9/27/74].

By November 16, my father had begun to hone in on that purpose, and he wrote this:

There seems to be a lot of trouble in Atlantic City High School and I'm going to write the principle and see if we can be of any help. Maybe they will let us speak to the students. They will talk to us better and easier than a cop or social worker and just maybe we can help straighten out some of the problems there. There has to be ways that the members of this program can be helpful in the communities [11/16/1974].

Within a year of enrolling in the program, he was voted as the Senior Coordinator for Alpha-Meta, which was essentially the program director. He wrote about this in his letter of November 14, 1974, two weeks shy of his one-year anniversary inside. What he wrote says alot about the time and the prison culture in 1974:

I was made Senior Co-Ordinator of Alpha-Meta, which means I am the program Director of Phase II. I have complete control and responsibility of all the members in the program. I am the very first white guy to ever hold the position. I couldn't believe that the staff, all Blacks, voted me into the position.

Because of his success and involvement in the drug program, my father eventually gained work experience in the field of addiction counseling, and he seized on opportunities to have any contact with the community — both in prison and outside — in a positive way.

Most assuredly, my father's letters illustrate the transformation of his mindset as he served his time. He found a passion helping others struggling with addiction, while simultaneously battling his own, and he talked about it a lot. In a letter to us that he wrote on

May 12, 1975, approximately eighteen (18) months into his sentence, he had this to say:

Later on this morning, I'm going to conduct the second session of a program for a local junior high school. We went to the school last time and it was 100% successful. Today, they are coming here to speak and to tour the prison and Alpha-Meta. I hope this one is just as effective. These kids and their parents are really concerned about the drug problem in their school and town. I love doing work like this. I want to find a job working with kids when I come home. I think it will also help me to stay away from drugs.

The rest of my father's letter from that spring morning told us, among other things, that he "*fell asleep all night with your letter next to me*", that he has been "*real good lately*", that he would probably never put a gun in his hand ever again after this "*whole trip*", that he had a staff meeting, school, group, a baseball game and then more studying to do that night. One of his most powerful expressions of the inner workings of his mind (and there were quite a few over time) that day was this: "*The main thing is that it may have stopped me from killing someone. It was eventually leading to that, you know?*" As always, there were reflections on his love for us and his intention to overcome the things in his life that led him to his addiction in the first place.

There were setbacks and struggles, to be sure. Being denied parole in March of 1975 was a devastating disappointment for him and he wasn't sure he was going to make it another year. His letters to my mother after he was denied, while we were in California visiting with her side of the family, are full of concern that I would think that he lied to me. On May 28, 1974, he had written, *"Pretty soon I'll quit this job and come home,"* thinking he would be home by my 5th birthday. However, not only did they deny him parole, but his rehearing was not scheduled for another year, so being home by April of the following year was no longer a possibility.

My father also had regular complaints about the people in the program using drugs, including some staff members. He encountered people that he very much wanted to punch but knew he couldn't. He found it *"easier adjusting to the streets"* on Fridays whenever he got furloughed than he did going back into the jail on Sundays. He watched people who came in after him get out before him, but he also pointed out that *"everyone that gets to go home means I'm that much closer to getting out myself. It's like walking home, every day I wake up is one day closer to home"* [12/17/74].

Even on his dark days, when the fears and frustrations, the anger and confusion, the despair and the sadness were evident in his writings, my father always made sure to infuse some positivity in order to cheer up his reader. He didn't hide the fact that doing the time was excruciating, but he also habitually remarked that there were "*better days ahead*". Whether he was doing it for his own sanity, or for my mom and me, I suppose we'll never know. But one thing is for sure, my father learned how to manage his emotions during that time period in his life, how to accept things that he could not change and how to resist the need for instant gratification so that he could find some peace of mind and some contentment in every situation. Basically, he learned how to deal with life without getting high.

One of the other benefits of being housed on "The Farm" was that my father did not have to be handcuffed in court when he appeared on charges for a separate incident for which he awaited sentencing while at Leesburg [8/10/74]. The possibility of a consecutive sentence from those other prior offenses weighed heavily on my father's mind until his court date arrived on September 20, 1974. Although he received another sentence of 3 to 5 years on those separate charges, my father was fortunate to have received a concurrent one that gave him credit for the time he had been serving since November 30, 1973. I have not seen the transcript of that proceeding, which would contain the rationale of the sentencing judge as to why he or she afforded my father some leniency, but I imagine that it had something to do with the fact that, by then, he had become one of the "Overseers" at

Alpha-Meta, and was beginning to do really good work with local, struggling youth.

Despite the good outcome, my father's correspondence to me and my mother the next day, on September 21, 1974 was highly reflective and very sad to read, given the deep remorse that he clearly felt:

> *The time is beginning to get to me. It's almost a year now. Mary, look at what I've done to my life. It's crazy. I've done so many crazy and stupid things in my life. I hurt you and Annmarie, your family, my family and mainly I almost ruined my life. I hope I'm able to resist drugs when I come home. It got terrible when I was home. All I did, everything I thought about was cocaine. I had such a bad habit, it drove me nuts.*

As usual, my father forged on, both in his letter and in his life. He ended the letter that day saying that he very much hoped that his furlough would be granted in December so that he could come home for Christmas. It was.

In his daily life, he immersed himself in school, enrolling every semester that they allowed him for as many credits as they would give him. He took so many credits that they ran out of classes to offer him. Eventually, he had to delay the achievement of his Associate's Degree until he could take classes on the street as part of another program that allowed him to attend college in person, on campus at Glassboro State College, which he began in June of 1975. By the time of his release in mid-1976, my father had many of the college credits that he needed for his Bachelor's Degree in Sociology and he also had a job lined up in addiction counseling at a place that launched his post-release career, Turning Point.

Peter and his mother, Ellen, at his college graduation

***

By Wayne Poppalardo

Dear Pete,

This is the letter I wish I had sent you sooner.

In July, 1976, you and I started at Turning Point Outpatient as drug abuse counselors. We bonded day one and shared an office we affectionately called "WOP", World Without Papers, honoring our common

Italian immigrant history. You are charismatic, so it wasn't unusual for everybody to instantly like you. Throughout the years you would say "WayneBo I tell you things I don't tell anyone else; you are the keeper of my secrets". And so it will remain, Pete. I will continue to keep your silent struggles, disappointments, and victories to myself and so continue to honor them. You are my closest and dearest friend. That doesn't change.

The unfolding and complexities of your character have been nothing less than remarkable. Some would say a miracle. Others would say there were contradictions in your character, but you always managed to make the whole work well.

And many might say confident, cocky, and charming. I would agree.

You are a wonderful combination of forces to be reckoned with and always respected. You are the person everyone knew would pick you up at 3 a.m. if you were walking down the road barefoot in a suit. I'm sure you remember that night.

You are always a gentleman and, when the situation called for it, sometimes not. You loved the ladies and they loved you back.

You are marshmallow soft inside and yet confrontational. I found you humble, but proud, and fearless unless you were camping. Always competitive even when playing spoons with my 5 year old daughter in the Dominican Republic. She beat you and your hands wore the scars from the combat.

You were present for Annmarie when she was an acting-out teenager and there for her today as an adult.

You were present, concerned and proud of your grandchildren, Evie and Nate. You described them as the most precious gift you ever received.

You were present for your first wife, Mary, your second wife Diana, and who would have been your third wife, Linda.

It was a mystery how you managed your relationships with many women over the years. You are able to maintain friendships with all the women in your life, even past the ending of a romantic relationship.

You continued to give to friends from the early years the loyalty and care they needed. You stuck through their illnesses, their challenges, and stayed by their side, whatever their needs.

Pete, you are truly magical, you have a real healing gift, with all the kids, the tough juveniles, and young people of all ages. You are passionate and invested in their well-being.

The bond between us remains, even 45 years later as we say goodbye. Goodbye, Pete, my closest and dearest friend.

***

By Wilda Connor

I first met Pete Gallione in the late 1970's. We met at a place called "Turning Point", the Camden County Center for Addictive Diseases in Blackwood, New Jersey. Pete was being sent to start up a "residential therapeutic community" and the office girls were none too happy! Up until then, our contact with drug addicts was limited to those with appointments to see counselors in an outpatient setting. But these counselors and addicts were very different. They were all ex-prison inmates, not our usual college educated, save the world, social worker, good guy types at all! We had our backs up and they knew it!

As the days went by and turned into months and years, however, we accepted each other. Many of Pete's treatment methods were controversial. He was meticulous in making sure things were kept clean and orderly, and God forbid shoes weren't lined up correctly! Off you go to the alley.

But Pete was so upfront, warm, and approachable that we all grew to love and respect him. If there was a problem, he would be the first one to offer help and advice. We kept in touch over the years, and I was so happy when he retired in Florida. We would talk on the phone a few times a year and I loved to hear his laugh and know that he was happy. My heart sank when I heard he was gone. A wonderful guy. I miss him and find it hard to believe he's not jumping in his pool as I type this. I think we helped him and he helped us. Just the way it should be, dear friend.

***

My father held a strong belief that addicts didn't need to be punished; they needed treatment. Some of my most vivid memories of my time with him when I was young involved watching him engage with the young residents in the Campus program that he directed just down the road from where he lived. Because the correctional system didn't sleep, we went to Campus a lot when I stayed with him. As a young person, almost as old as the juveniles in the program, it didn't seem to be so much of an institution where kids were committed — though it was — as it seemed to be a school with kids who lived there. I loved it because it had sports fields and common areas where people spent time together in groups.

Campus was very different from my school, a parochial one in North Jersey. Recess at my school was played on blacktop every day; Campus had greenhouses. We wore Catholic school uniforms and they wore monochrome pants and shirts. We learned core academic subjects; they learned core academic subjects *and* how to manage their emotions and their addictions.

The young residents all clearly had a good rapport with my father at Campus, even though he could have made any one of their lives miserable at any moment by returning them to traditional juvenile detention if they didn't follow the program. Certainly, there were kids that were perhaps new to the program and wouldn't make eye contact with him yet; but those who knew my father, as far as I could see, responded well to him. For sure, everyone seemed to be on their best behavior when the boss and his young daughter walked around the grounds. There was an energy about the place that felt safe and good for you, even though you could sense the struggles that the residents were obviously enduring. To me, it seemed like a place where someone could get well.

The older I got, the more I understood the circumstances of the juveniles who were sent by the court to my father's drug program at Campus. Many of those circumstances called for the sense of security that both the program and my father's hugs provided. In him, and in his staff, they found not only treatment counselors but quite a few people who had sat where they presently sat and, therefore, could genuinely relate to them. I saw this in the way that they naturally opened up, engaged him, and seemed calm in his presence. They were going through difficult times, and so had my father and many of those who worked with him at an earlier point in their lives. I would venture to bet that I had one of the more interesting "bring your child to work day" venues.

***

By Astrid M. Lee

It is hard to believe and even more difficult to accept that Pete is gone. I am not sure where to start.

Words cannot express what Pete meant to me. I have delayed writing this because I just could not get over the loss and sadness, but then I realized that I should be celebrating the life he lived. I know without a doubt that he would not want to be here if he was not 100% himself.

I have always known that God sent me to work with Pete. He was such a blessing to my life. He was so much more than just my boss, you see. God knew this man would redirect my life and give me a different perspective on how I viewed the world. I was a negative thinker, always seeing the glass half empty and carrying negative thoughts and animosity with me about how I was treated as a child. I will never forget him telling me, "No one can make you feel anything. That is your choice."

Let me tell you how annoyed I was because I just did not understand that concept. Let's just say from that point on, he would explain a new way of thinking and redirecting my thoughts. This new way of thinking gave me power over my life and changed the trajectory of my future. When I met Pete, I was on the verge of being a single Mom. He was ALWAYS there for me, talking me off the ledge.

He was a mentor to my sons, from counseling them when they would get in some situation at school to giving them mock interviews when needed. They always looked forward to coming to work with me and interacting with "Mr. Pete". When we got our first dog, they had to take him to meet Mr. Pete (he was such a dog person). Pete taught us how to train our Coby and even pet-sat for us when we would go away on vacation.

Pete became an intricate part of my family. Everyone who had the pleasure of meeting him was saddened by the news. I can truly say that no one has impacted my life the way Pete has. This void will be felt for a long time to come.

***

By Colleen Toner

It was the summer of 1988 when I first met Peter Gallione. He was part of a four-person team that conducted my interview for a position with the Department of Corrections in a newly developed juvenile (female) inpatient substance abuse program in Camden County.

Fresh out of college ready to change the world, Pete's first inclination after the interview was that he would be "surprised" if I lasted a couple of months. LOL. Well, thankfully he was incorrect. I credit both Pete and Michelle, whose compassion, love, and concern supported my growth and longevity. When Pete and I would reminisce about "the interview", we enjoyed sharing the story with others followed by a few good laughs.

I am very blessed to have had Pete as a supervisor, mentor, advocate, coworker, and friend. I learned so much from his commitment to recovery and taking that commitment to task in his daily interactions with youth and staff. Pete touched so many lives and accomplished so much in the field of substance abuse for the JJC.

After Brad and I moved our home to Naples, Florida in 2015, we had the opportunity to visit Pete regularly. It became a given that in the winter months, usually in either February or March, during Michelle's visits to Naples, we would either plan to drive to

Pompano to see Pete or Pete would travel across Alligator Alley to the west coast of Florida to visit us.

I was initially shocked and amazed seeing Pete's backyard for the first time. He actually planted beautiful tropical flowers and a banana tree surrounding his pool! I didn't think Pete had a green thumb, but his plants grew into a lush tropical oasis. Boy, did he love his pool and living in Florida!!

I recall Pete mentioning during our visits together through the years that he always thanked God for each year he was given on this Earth. He said, "it's a gift" and "god willing" we would meet again next year.

Our last visit together was in Naples on March 4, 2020. I am so happy we were able to see each other before the world went into quarantine. Our last visit together was truly a gift.

...Miss you dearly, Pete.

***

By Frances Micelli

My connection with your dad, on paper, was one of treatment counselor versus parole officer. But Pete was a partner to me every step of the way. He cared about our mutual clients. He became their biggest cheerleader for their recovery. Even when we disagreed on something, we worked it out. We grew to respect each other over the 30-some years we worked together or saw each other at mutual conferences or joint meetings once our careers took us up the ladder. We trusted each other, and so often referred or consulted with each other. We loved that we both were Italian. He was famous for dating and once came to my house with a date who I worked with and who lived in my town. He liked that I approved. Our relationship on Facebook just supported and honored the respect we had for each other. My story is not specific incidents but a lifetime of professional closeness that I will always cherish.

***

For many, connecting with my father after his recovery was not only fortunate, it was potentially life-saving. For the latter two-thirds of his life, he redeemed himself on a daily basis by paying forward the blessings, the lessons, and the coping skills that he had learned and honed throughout his recovery. He never, ever took his life and his freedom for granted again. There was only one reason that he would ever let himself wind up in prison again, and fortunately no one harmed any of his loved ones during his lifetime in a way that put him in that position. For sure, he made that clear to each and every person that I chose to date.

My father had paid his dues and had personally done the work of rehabilitating himself and therefore possessed the wherewithal to lead others on their own path toward rehabilitation.

***

By Michelle McCreary

What can I say about Pete Gallione? Quite simply, I am here today because I had the good fortune to meet him. In December of 1980, I had agreed to go to a program called Turning Point. It was located in Blackwood, New Jersey and Pete was the director. I was a heroin addict, having just detoxed for the second time.

Though I had only arrived on December 3rd, I was allowed to go home for Christmas. The last thing I said to my boyfriend when he dropped me back off was that I would not admit to having gotten drunk. Once everyone had returned, Pete held a quick group, asking each of us if we had used any substances while we were out. Without hesitation, I said "yes". I had known him for three weeks and discovered that I could not lie to his face. I was, at that time, a poor excuse for a human being. I was undependable, totally self-absorbed, and most definitely a liar. But I could not lie to Pete.

Turning Point was an incredible place. A therapeutic community designed with love and a sincere desire to help us overcome our addictions as Pete had overcome his. There was something very special about Pete Gallione. He was intuitive and supportive, but never a pushover.

My next significant interaction with Pete occurred several months into my stay. As a self-admission, I decided I was ready to go home. I knew what I needed to do. Pete took the time to sit with me in the cafeteria. I don't recall all of the conversation, but I remember that he suggested to me that if I left then, it would be yet another thing I did not complete. That conversation changed my mind. And in helping me change my mind, Pete changed the course of my life. I completed Turning Point after thirteen months of residential treatment and six months of aftercare.

About six months later, I went to work in the same building with Pete. Over the next four and a half years, I was employed by the county and, with other alumni, started an association to help others. Pete was naturally working right alongside of us. The organization eventually folded and I moved back to the shore.

In 1987, I was hired by Klaus Aschim to work at Camden House under the Department of Corrections, Juvenile Division. Pete had since left Turning Point and was also working for DOC. For the next twenty-five years, I worked in Juvenile Justice, most of them with Pete. He was my boss and my mentor, but most importantly, my dear friend.

There are so many memories, it is hard to name only a few. Some that really stand out are: the pool parties at Ray's house; the time Pete decided that he, Bob, and I were going to leave work and drive to Queens to see the Mets game; the trip to Cape Hatteras, North Carolina; the many, many stops at Dunkin Donuts for coffee; watching Pete run group (he was the best); calling Pete when I needed help with a controversy; having lunch with Pete and Colleen every winter in Florida, sometimes on the East Coast, sometimes on the West Coast, sometimes joined by others.

A friendship of almost forty years... priceless. I could talk to Pete, really talk. He pulled no punches and accepted no excuses. He was exactly what one needs in a friend. I miss him terribly. On May 6, I had yet another birthday, and for the first time in as long as I can remember, Pete did not call.

***

By Frani Williams
"My Mentor Pete Gallione — Gone but Never Forgotten"

The beginning of 2021 has been tough, and not having my friend and mentor Pete to talk to about it, makes it even tougher. I know he would tell me, "if anybody can get through this, you can." I know this because he has told me that so many times before.

I met Pete in 1987. I was a graduate of the Turning Point drug program. From day one, he commanded my respect and love because he always put a mirror in front of me to see myself, my flaws, and my worth. He became my boss in that same year at the Campus Youth Advocate Program (CYAP) and Campus girls. He taught me early on to press my way, never let anyone's actions cripple me, and don't make excuses. He taught me to be in charge of my destiny, and by God's grace and direction, I was.

In 1988, someone told him I was using drugs on the job, and I wasn't. I told him repeatedly I was not, but he asked me to resign and I did. In that same year, I relapsed. Pete didn't realize that the job was my life and my first chance at living life on life's terms. I went to prison and continued to keep in touch, always telling him that I was not using when he asked me to resign. I prayed one day he would believe me.

When I got out of prison, he was the first person I called and asked for a job. He told me to get a job on my own and work there and keep checking in. I got a great job working for Family Services, and we kept in touch over the next five years. I frequently spoke with him and Michelle McGlue, my other mentor. I told him of every goal I had reached and every promotion, until one day I got my heart up and asked him and Michelle if I could come back. Praise God, they made a way for me to come back. I took a $5,000 pay cut to become a youth worker, but it was worth it just to be home again under people who knew and understood me.

The rest is a history that neither of us could have predicted. I excelled greatly, and he was always in my corner, even when I became his superior. He said to me, "I knew you would do well, you have surpassed me. I never thought you would achieve the things you have achieved!" The first was the development of the DOVES program. I was asked 3 times to develop that program before I said yes. Pete had faith and confidence in me that I didn't have. He said, "You are the only one that can do this because of what you have been through in your life." He taught me how to be a supervisor, create a therapeutic community, and empower people to change. It first started with an illusion of power that they would grow into. He taught me everything I know about the disease of addiction and we built a model program that is still up and running to this very day!

I was promoted from DOVES and went on to the executive offices. After that, I was asked to supervise the only female prison for juveniles in the state of New Jersey. This position meant that I would be supervising correctional officers along with civilian staff in a secure facility. Yes, me, an ex-inmate. Well, that was not happening. The ish hit the fan. I came into work one day and my mug shot and criminal history was pasted all over the building. I was so upset, because now everyone knew I was an ex-offender. Don't get me wrong, my superiors knew but, now ___everyone___ knew. Apparently, some correctional officers did not want an ex-offender being their boss. I was hurt to my core. For some reason, I thought I had arrived somewhere and their actions took me back to feeling like that broken woman who was a drug addict and prisoner. I felt helpless and hopeless.

So, I called Pete crying my eyes out, and WHAT DID HE SAY? "SO, THEY OUTTED YOU?" I was fired up mad and beet-faced red and I am dark skinned! He said, "What they did was about their insecurities, not yours, what do you have to be ashamed of?" He put a mirror back in my face. "After all you done, he said, you gonna let that ish bother you?" Man, I miss him.

See, that's the beauty of Pete, if he loved you (and I know he loved me), he would never let you wallow in self-pity. He would say what you didn't want to hear, but what he knew would propel you forward. So what I did next was got up and fought, and I've been fighting ever since.

We have always stayed connected, whether it was playing Words with Friends or just talking. He kept telling me to come to Florida to visit, and write my book. He told me many times how proud he was of me and I loved him for it. I never told him this but, he was the father I never had. My heart is truly broken that he is not here. I will always love him and remember him, and feel in certain parts of my life, he is supposed to be there.

I love you, Pete. I will write the book and you will be all in it. Rest well, my friend and mentor. Your voice will never be silent in my head or heart. I will miss you so very much because you taught me everything I know about recovery and how to help others. Thank you! Your legacy forever lives on in me and all the lives you have touched. Gone, but never forgotten.

Love, respect, and honor,
Francine Williams, "Frani", or "kiddo"

***

By Karen Sellers Hicks

It was the summer of 1980. I had just turned 21, but life was standing still, as I had nowhere to run. But run I did, right into a brick wall. It was the lowest point of my life as I waited to stand in front of a judge for the accidental death of my baby boy. I was horrified, scared, and guilt-ridden, but then I met Peter Gallione. I was admitted to Turning Point for exactly 106 days until my incarceration. On that 105th day I demanded to see Pete, not my counselor or any one else.

As I sat across from this man, arms crossed, slouched, and my legs crossed like a guy, Pete instructed me to "sit up like a lady". And I've been sitting up like a lady ever since! I asked what I should expect as I entered prison. He told me 3 things: "mind your business, don't snitch, and keep a low profile". This advice would get me through some tough days. I have never forgotten a word he spoke to me. His demeanor, his attitude, and mostly his love and empathy are what pulled me in to believe every word he said to me. Pete lifted me to a higher understanding of what I was meant to be. Pete told me how he lives his life, free of alcohol and drugs, and he convinced me that I could do it too.

Now I'd love to say I was this great success from that day on, but that would take away all of my life's lessons. The point is for all my days, Peter's words would linger in my mind. Pete had a gentle but stern way of being brutally honest and supporting no negative contracts. He taught me to be in the moment without holding back. Most of all he loved me, broken and lost, with such deep compassion.

How do I measure the value of a man that helped mold and change my life? More importantly, what can I do to show my gratitude? Simply living the life God intended for me to live. I saw my success every time Pete's face would light up when I would see him through the years.

Pete, I will never say good-bye. I have loved, respected, and admired you for so, so long. I miss you! And I want you to know how very grateful I am for you. Thank you is so trivial, but also so deep, and I am thankful for having had you in my life.

***

By Anonymous

Off the record and for your eyes only[6]... your Dad was the key that got me through a very difficult time in my life. Following surgery, I was in great pain for years. I was encouraged to take and freely supplied with oxycontin by my doctor. I, fortunately, never abused it so would have to endure periods of withdrawal every day. After a couple years of this, I tried to stop, but was not able to on my own.

One day, I ran into your Dad and began to talk to him about this. Pete took me into a room and listened

---

[6] Published anonymously with the author's permission.

for a while. What happened next is not what I expected. Being a counselor myself, I constantly "grouped" on myself everyday — asking the hard questions and trying to be honest with myself. I expected this same process with Pete, but that is not how it went. I honestly cannot do justice to what your Dad did, but he took me down a path I had never been on and one I could not do myself. The process was what I needed. I took a week off soon after that and got myself cleaned up, and never went back. I will be forever grateful to your Dad for that, for giving so deeply of himself to me. He saved my life.

***

The connections that my father made in his professional life were equally matched by the ones that he made during this era in his personal life. As many of the contributors to this project know, my father's proclivities in love were… notable. He was both a lover and a fighter and, in the early days, being faithful was not among his best attributes. Eventually, as my father's sobriety enabled him to relearn the value of relationships, he became someone who could love better, who could be relied upon and who many trusted infinitely.

***

By Diana Di Bona

Peter's Second Wife and Annmarie's Stepmother

My first impression of Pete was when I met him at a club one night. He looked like he had just walked out of a scene from Goodfellas… long black leather trench coat… piercing eyes. The truth is under that streetwise tuff guy exterior was a man with a heart as big as his beautiful dimpled smile. Little did I know that he would end up becoming my husband for the next 25 years and, even after our divorce, one of my closest friends for the rest of his life. Whatever challenges were thrown his way he handled with his amazing coping skills, which he also shared with so many people. His love and dedication to helping others became his journey to what he called "paying back", but in reality, he went above and beyond to all who reached out to him. He opened his heart to my nephews and we were able to provide a stable and loving home for them during the most challenging times in their lives, which was truly a gift to me… I will be forever grateful to him for providing wonderful memories of love and family.

Throughout most of my adult life, Pete has been there in one way or another, playing key roles during times of extreme sadness, loss, and life challenges with words of wisdom and just knowing he was there to catch you… and also my most amazing and joy-filled moments. He was gifted with the best sense of humor and quick wit and could draw you in with his beautiful energy.

I was Blessed to have shared a big part of my life journey with him.

***

My father was married to my mother from April of 1969 until January of 1971, after a tumultuous twelve-year relationship. He was married to my stepmother, Diana, with whom I always shared a loving relationship, from February of 1980 until March of 2003. At the moment my father died, my mother and I were in flight to South Florida, hoping that, by some miracle, we would get to see him again. Diana picked us up from the airport and took us to the hospital, where his body remained. I could not help but feel immense gratitude sitting in the car with both of them while my father's spirit was transitioning. That car contained the three women who loved my father the longest throughout his lifetime. Because of the relationships that he created with each of them, those three women — his two wives and his daughter — could carry the gargantuan weight of his loss together.

Many others loved my father throughout his lifetime, and he loved many of them in return.

***

By Janet

Pete Gallione entered my life like a strong, quiet tornado. A force of nature. We met at a meeting that he reluctantly attended; I was DYFS - he was JJC; agencies that shared mutual disdain. I was chairing a multi-disciplinary Southern Regional Steering Committee to explore child deaths related to parental substance abuse. Pete thought it was likely totally "bureaucratic BS". After avoiding these meetings for several months, he showed up one day, in full "attitude".

At the end of that first meeting, Pete Gallione introduced himself to me — and then offered to carry out boxes to my car — and we began to know each other. Over the course of the next several months (he rarely missed a meeting) we talked regularly by phone. We shared a deep, mutual passion for children and adolescents and, it turned out, a mutual disdain for governmental disregard for the same population. We would spend hours, late into the night, on the phone sharing our intense feelings and, as these feelings shifted into our personal connection, we began a personal relationship.

We were unlikely partners; Pete, a "city boy" found himself in places like Vermont (my idea) where he declared openly to strangers on a hike: "I don't know how I got here! I don't go into nature!" I found his openness and honesty to be extraordinary and beautifully vulnerable, especially for a 'tough guy'. He would easily and openly tell me how he had to get up extra early to try on outfits before our meetings to make sure he looked 'good enough'. These were incredible paradoxes in a man as 'tough' as Pete Gallione.

And Pete was tough.

He was a man that loved intensely. I have absolutely no doubt that he would have killed for those he loved, as he openly declared.

And Pete was vulnerable.

Regarding feelings of uncontrolled emotion he would openly say things like: "I feel like I was dropped on my head upside down in Africa and have no idea where I am."

And, years after our most intimate connection was too hard to maintain, our heart connection continued. And that is what I most want to say about my experience of Pete Gallione.

I loved Pete — and I continue to love Pete. I always knew that his love for me — and for all of those he loved — was real and unending. I could hear it in his voice and feel it in his energy.

Pete Gallione's heart was pure — huge and pure. And for all he loved, he continues to hold them close.

***

By Robin Nighland

I think about your dad all the time. I remember the first time I ever saw him at the JJC. He was so charismatic and he really cared about the kids. He also didn't like to follow the rules and did whatever it took to help his boys. We hit it off right away and I used to look forward to him visiting my division. I met him about 17 years ago. I can honestly say I have never met anyone like him. I would always ask him if he stopped smoking and he would always say "yes" and start laughing. Then he would say to me "you have to die of something". I would tell him he needed to eat more vegetables and he would laugh and say "that's never going to happen," as he was making his tuna and egg salad.

The time we spent together I will always cherish, and I was so happy to meet you and your children. He will always hold a special place in my heart and I really miss talking to him. So many times I find myself saying "if I can only talk to Pete." You and your children were the loves of his life. I have wonderful memories of him and the fun times we spent together. Your dad used to say "I don't know why God is so good to me." God bless all of you and remember your dad is always with you.

***

By Lisa Marie Russo
"Me and Pete"

My cousin, Linda Bompensa, first dated Pete briefly in the seventies. I didn't know him then, as I was only about twelve years old. But Linda inhabited an impossibly glamorous world; she was a model, worked at the Merry-Go-Round in the Deptford Mall, and had a business card that said "Troubleshooter". Surely, Linda and Pete drank cocktails and disco danced at the Deptford Tavern. Much later, I learned that my Aunt Tootsie thought this was an unholy alliance, which only added an extra touch of frisson to the tale of the short-lived dalliance.

In October 2003, my 38-year-old brother Dean died in his sleep. Devastated, I returned to New Jersey from my home in London. Linda delivered my mom's eulogy for Dean. A devout Catholic and a reader at church, she was a natural. At the wake, I learned that the romance with Pete had been reignited. They bumped into each other at a party and the passion ripped through them like a wildfire. Linda's marriage would end and life would never be the same again.

I met Pete in the flesh en route to Midnight Mass. Linda would be reading, but she didn't want to draw attention to the relationship, so I'd be sitting with him. We rendezvoused at the Olympia in Vineland. A Greek restaurant — it added to the mythology of this man and this love story, on this most sacred and star-filled night. He burst in and hugged me tight, "I'm so sorry to hear about your brother." He recognized the rawness of my grief, and told me about the untimely losses in his own family. We connected.

Pete and Linda were living together soon after. But within a year, she was diagnosed with lung cancer. I raced back in April of 2005 and spent the last five days of her life together with Linda and Pete. He looked after her lovingly, with deep kindness and compassion. Although Aunt Tootsie and Uncle Dom accepted Pete and came to adore him as well, there were still family tensions. It was left to me to negotiate deathbed visits for Linda, and Pete said, "Lisa, you are like Switzerland." I loved this idea and I still declare it (and credit him) when I have a tricky business deal to sort out. When my own mother didn't feel well enough to attend Linda's funeral at the last minute, I was conflicted. I turned to Pete, "What would Linda say?" He thought about it and said, "That's OK." I realized he understood the boundaries of grieving parents. He understood forgiveness and, of course in his own life, redemption.

I loved keeping in touch with Pete. Seeing how he rebuilt his shattered world with the love and support of his family, and the sunshine of Florida. And he gave me advice on dealing with addiction in my own circles. I loved that he posted his feelings about Trump so voraciously, in a state which looked the other way. His posts were smart and funny and irreverent. And then, suddenly, there was that heartbreaking post on his page. He was gone. Like his friends, I wished he was here to see the nail-biting, jubilant way Philly brought home Pennsylvania for the new president. A win he had fought and prayed for. And yet, we knew he was up there, dancing on the clouds, beaming love and light and laughs down to the rest of us.

I'll never forget Pete, he made a real difference in my life.

***

Prior to his retirement, my father worked extremely hard. The requirements of his job meant that he was always on call. Since the individuals in many of his programs throughout the years were court-ordered to be there, they were actually sentenced to his custody. I distinctly recall several times over the years when inmates escaped and our family time or my father's sleep was interrupted. Those calls were extremely upsetting to my father, because it meant that the system had failed one of the individuals in his care. He knew full well that if one of them left, they likely would be using drugs in the near future and that potentially meant devastating consequences for that person and their loved ones. He wanted the same success that he himself experienced for every one of those offenders, and because he was the head of the program, my father took some responsibility for that outcome whenever it occurred.

Though my father did a lot of good for others, he still had his own vices, and no accurate telling of his life would be complete without mentioning them. He never could kick the cigarette habit, he struggled with his weight, and he spent a fair amount of his free time during those years gambling. Whenever I would nag him about any of the above, he would respond: "I kicked cocaine and heroin. Let me have these things." And so, believing I had a choice, I did.

He knew where to draw the line, however. I remember an eye-opening interaction that I had with him when I was in my mid-twenties. A good friend of mine was in a band and my dad, who knew her, came to the club to see the show. During a break, a group was heading out back. I let him know what was happening and asked, kind of hesitantly, if he wanted to join. I knew by then that he was a proponent of marijuana legalization and, in my mind, it was just a plant that did less harm than alcohol, which had been flowing freely throughout that club from top to bottom all night. Marijuana had never been my father's problem, in any event.

I remember my dad looking at me, smiling but very serious. He said, "Annmarie, I am still the same addict today as I was twenty years ago. I can't ever do that." Two decades later, I was naive enough to assume that my father had such a handle on his addiction to cocaine and heroin that a little "reefer" — as he called it — couldn't possibly knock him off his game. I was wrong and he set me straight. In that moment, I came to understand his addiction even more. He was still, after all of those years clean, taking his recovery day by day.

Despite his control when it came to drugs, genetics and other aspects of my father's lifestyle caused him to suffer three heart attacks before the final ones that eventually took his life. Each time, he observed the early signs and, each time, took himself to the hospital, where his life was saved. The first one occurred when I was a college student in Miami. He and Diana's family were driving back to New Jersey after we all attended a wedding in Florida. He actually felt the symptoms while driving on I-95, found the nearest hospital, and drove the van directly there. I spent several nights cramming for my finals in that hospital in Central Florida that week, and with a mind that was full of worry, received the lowest marks of my college career that semester.

My father had several heart procedures over the years and required daily medication and regular visits to his cardiologist after that. He knew that his heart would eventually fail him, and so he was sure to maximize his time on earth while it lasted. A heart attack would be quick and, to him, the thought of becoming sick and possibly dependent upon others for his own care, was a dreadful alternative. He joked often that he just wanted "that big one" to put a period at the end of his life story. He had a plan in the event of the former scenario, and he had my assurance that I would be there for him if and when the time ever came.

For the good of us all, that event did not come to pass and my father outlived all expectations and sailed smoothly into his retirement. He worked for the State of New Jersey in one capacity or another from the time he was committed to the prison system in 1973 until his official retirement in 2007. When he retired, he had ascended to the role of Substance Abuse Administrator of the Juvenile Justice Commission, working directly under the New Jersey Attorney General. He had to wear a suit and tie in those days and he inherited a daily commute to Trenton, which he deplored, but he knew that his impact could be felt on a wider scale in that particular bureaucratic role. He often shared how much he missed working in the programs, counseling kids and coordinating a staff that was working, hands-on, in the treatment realm. That was where he felt most useful. But in the statewide administrator role, my father was able to implement drug treatment plans on a grander scale throughout New Jersey and this, to him, was worth the drawbacks and the red tape that he associated with it.

I tried to express how impressed I was with my father's professional work at his retirement dinner in 2007, but I failed. My speech on his behalf at that event, in front of 75-100 people, was a blubbering mess. I could not contain my emotions that day (despite all that he taught me), and so it was difficult for me to convey my words. My father, as any good father would, came up on stage to save me. He knew that the reason why it was overwhelming for me was because I was overcome with pride and gratitude for all of his accomplishments. Those accomplishments included staying true to the promises that he had made me long ago in his letters from prison. From that commitment, he never retired.

***

PART THREE
THE LATER YEARS

If the first third of his life was damaging and the middle of his life redeeming, then the final third of my father's life can be narrowed down to this singular word: *contentment.* My father's recovery enabled him to develop, keep, nourish, repair, and reignite relationships and to enjoy those bonds in his later years, when he had so much more room to breathe. During his retirement, he spent many days connecting with family and friends through visits, phone calls, emails, Facebook, and personal visits. He purchased a home that provided a tropical and peaceful oasis, not just for him every day, but for so many others who enjoyed time there with him. He used to say that he *"bought a backyard and the house just came with it."* There was something very special about the near-constant gentle breeze that blew through his back patio and the way the sun lit up his yard in the daytime and the way the moon washed over it at night. Mostly, I think his place was healing because of the energy that he created there.

Relationships were so important to my father that he maintained deep connections with people even when traditional bonds were broken. In addition to honoring his post-marriage relationships with both my mother and my stepmother and their extended families, my father also continued to nourish the bond that he developed with my own husband and his family, even long after our marriage ended. Once you became family to my father, you remained family to my father.

***

<u>By Ron Jensen</u>

I would like to have had one more conversation with you. I think I'll still have those imagined conversations you have with someone even when they're not present, but if I could have told you one thing before you left this world, I would have said 'thank you'. You knew that I loved you and cherished our relationship, but if there's one thing I could have expressed to you, it would be my gratitude for the love and the lessons you've given to me and those who knew you.

I'm sure you wanted to have some more time here, if for nothing else but to see Evie and Nate grow into adulthood. But in a strange, comforting way, I think that you were okay with going when you did. You always thought that you were living on borrowed time. Your genetics, your health history, your wild youth — you had a lot of reasons to believe that you were lucky to reach your 70s. Maybe it was luck or good fortune, or maybe it's because some higher power wanted you to spread your lessons and love to as many people as possible. Whatever it was, the world was a better place with you in it, and you made sure of that. Thank you for that.

I don't think you left anything on the table. You let everyone know how you felt about them with every Christmas card, birthday wish, and every simple 'I love you' when saying goodbye on the phone. I never had to wonder how you felt about me. Thank you for that.

You were a father figure to me, Dad. You showed me the powerful, loving message of a big hug. You taught me to be unafraid to examine my own feelings. And you modeled unconditional love that I'm still learning lessons from. However, there are some things that we will never see eye to eye on — your Mets and my Phillies, your Giants and my Eagles, your Junior Mints and my Peppermint Patties...

Your life has been a fascinating journey, and I'm very curious to read the other contributions in this tribute to you. It's a life that you had before I knew you, and hearing about you from the people who were with you at different points along that journey will help me know you better and appreciate you even more. I've always thought that you were living proof that with determination and discipline, anyone can make themselves into what they want to be. As a person and as a counselor, you knew that whatever changes need to happen must start from within. It's a lesson we're all told but rarely do we have to dig as deep down as you did in order to realize what that truly means. You are someone who I look to when I need help finding my own inner strength. Thank you for that.

There's a certain amount of consolation I feel when it comes to your passing. I'm confident that you were living the life you wanted to live. Your family, your friends, your life as a retiree in Florida — all of it. I believe that you were where you wanted to be. I'm sure you wanted a little more time in this world, and the opportunity to say goodbye to the people in your life. But maybe because you realized the fragility of life, you made sure to let the people you loved know that you cared about and appreciated them. I know I felt that from you. Again, thank you for that.

My heart aches at your loss. I will miss you immensely. I'll miss seeing you during the holidays, complaining about the cold. I'll miss a quick text or call after an Eagles-Giants game, and your ever-present Werthers. I'll miss you calling me 'son', because that was a unique place that I held among your family and loved ones. I'll miss seeing you beam with pride at Evie and Nate. Please know that the lessons you imparted to me and Annmarie will continue to benefit your grandchildren—

To listen to others.

Know yourself.

Be resilient.

Respect others but don't put up with their shit, and don't let them bullshit themselves.

Let the people you love know how you feel about them.

It's a legacy that I'm certain you wanted, and one that you are proud of.

Thank you for that.

***

<u>*By Lynn Jensen*</u>

When I think of Pete, the first thing that comes to mind is the big bear hugs I would get from him. We only saw him twice a year after he moved to Florida, but whenever I saw him he had a smile on his face. Pete would call me on Mother's Day, which was so thoughtful. He'd say, "I wouldn't forget you." He was always so nice. We were part of an exclusive four-person club, being grandparents to Evie and Nate. I will miss seeing him, and miss those great hugs.

With all my love, Lynn

***

By Ron Jensen, Sr.

Me and Pete had a friendly sports rivalry going on. He was a Mets and Giants fan, and I was a Phillies and Eagles fan. When he came up, we would bust on each other depending on who was playing a good game. Or not playing a good game. It won't be as much fun anymore when those teams play each other. The one thing we both liked is being grandfathers to Evie and Nate.

Left to right: Terry Watson, Ron Jensen Sr., Lynn Jensen, Peter Gallione, Nathaniel Jensen, Ron Jensen, Eve Jensen, Annmarie Gallione, and Mary Gallione

***

By Nancy Martini
Mary's Younger Sister

In 1970 B.A. (before Annmarie), I remember lots of one-on-one time with my brother-in-law. Until the last time I spoke with him, 5 days before his beautiful soul left this earth, he always called me his sister-in-law, and vice versa. I'm guessing my sister was out somewhere, because when I recently told her this memory, she shouted a bit and cursed him, as usual… we all knew she loved him more than she cursed him, but an outsider would think she hated his guts.

Anyway, in 1970 there was this cylinder bolster which my sister used to put her bed pillows in to make it look perfect (does that surprise anyone?). Well, when she wasn't home, Peter would put me inside this cylinder and roll me all around the house. I'd laugh and laugh…Then he'd put me on his shoulders to watch football with plenty of jumping around and horsey rides on his back. Perhaps I have him to thank for my love for roller coasters and crazy rides! Can you imagine more fun as a 4 year-old?!

Then one day, I remember going to the Grant Street apartment with my mother and refusing to get out of the car. She tricked me by saying we were going to see MY baby, "Rie Rie", but I saw "his" car in the parking lot and wasn't having it. I didn't know why — I just knew my sister was hurting and it was his fault. I guess that shit was born into my Italian blood.

It truly took many years for me to form another bond with him. Notice I didn't say I forgave or forgot, but I did love him. He was my family after all. I do remember picnics with Peter, my sister, Ellie Pooh, and Annmarie in Leesburg over the next few years.

Then in 1976, I remember going for a ride and into some kind of store with him. He saw a friend who was really happy to see him (after all these years). The friend asked where he'd been and I remember him looking at me, then back at his friend, and he whispered "I was in P-R-I-S-O-N." When we got back to the car, I said, "Peter, you do know I'm 10 right??" P-R-I-S-O-N helped him in many ways, but not so much in adding the years to my age! He did emerge a much better man, one I'm so very proud of, but I'll let those who knew that side and reaped those benefits tell that part of his story.

***

<u>By Charles Martini</u>

Mary's brother

Spoken by Charles, written by Annmarie

Our family moved to Teaneck, New Jersey from 118th Street and 1st Ave in New York City on August 1, 1958. Not long after, Peter and his family moved to the neighborhood. I think that I first met him when my cousins and I were playing stickball in the street. but our friendship truly developed when we were in Boy Scouts together. We didn't last long in Scouts — it wasn't really for us — but we did have some fun times.

We used to stop for ice cream at the Carvel on Teaneck Road walking back from meetings, and I remember one particular memory that stands out vividly.

We were doing something that we shouldn't have been doing and a police officer stopped to talk to us. The officer asked for our names, and Peter and I were being difficult about giving them up. A third boy who was with us told the officer Peter's name, and being ratted on didn't sit well with Peter, even then. Peter thought I told on him at first and the next thing I knew, I had his ice cream all over me. Once I told him that it wasn't me, Peter took the ice cream and smeared it all over the kid who <u>did</u> snitch on him. We all had a good laugh after that incident.

My cousin Anthony became good friends with Peter too, and sometimes both of them would stay over at our house. I recall one time when Peter was over and his mother, who I always called Aunt Ellen, couldn't find him and came down the street calling his name. My mother, Anna, who always looked for any excuse to stop ironing, went outside to invite Ellen in. After that, Anna and Ellen were like Mutt and Jeff. They became good friends even before Peter and Mary became close and remained that way until Ellen died.

My sister, Mary, began seeing Peter and I always thought they would wind up together. Even after they divorced, I always thought they would remarry. Their mutual stubbornness got in the way, though. I have always considered Peter my brother-in-law, whether they were together or not.

I remember a time when Aunt Ellen was in the hospital and I rode my bike all the way from Congress Avenue in Teaneck to Englewood Hospital to see her. Both Aunt Ellen and Peter were upset with me, but I wanted to see her and, at the time, I had no way else to get to the hospital. There was no one like Aunt Ellen.

Another memory that I distinctly remember occurred sometime after the Fall of 1964. We were living on Bradley Avenue in Bergenfield by then. Mary and Peter were split at the time and Mary went on a date with someone else. I remember that it was a Friday night, because I was home alone. (My mother played cards in the city on Friday nights and my father stayed out too, so we were always flying solo on Fridays.)

Peter had discovered Mary on the date and followed her home, yelling at her. His friend, Buzzy, was with him. Peter came into the house and Buzzy tried to follow him. I didn't mind Peter coming in, but I would not let Buzzy follow. I remember that Buzzy threatened to hit me but Peter wouldn't allow it. Eventually, in order to get them to leave, I picked up an outdoor trash can and threw it at both of them. This story was recounted over the years as the night that I used a trash can as a weapon to protect my sister. Peter got a kick out of that.

Despite everything, I never had any doubt that Peter would turn out ok. I always believed that he would make something of himself. As I said, I also always thought that he and my sister would remarry, but they were both so stubborn and independent. Even though they fought a lot and complained about each other a lot, I knew they loved each other and would always be there for each other.

Peter has always held, and always will hold, a very special place in my heart and mind.

***

By Pam Messina
Mary's cousin

So Peter and I first met under not the best conditions. Mary, Ralph, and Peter attended my cheering competition (which we won) in Dumont. I had never met Peter, but he had been sitting and talking to Ralph's ex-girlfriend the whole time. Just a bit awkward, although she and I were friends. Then I went on to babysitting Annmarie in the apartments on Grant Street with Ralph. Peter got into some bad choices that left Mary and Annmarie alone a lot and that made me upset, and Peter became less than my favorite — after all, Annmarie was "my baby" at the time.

Fast forward and Peter certainly turned his life around and made amends with all. I then admired him for helping youth with addictions and so much more. I will always miss Christmas Eve when he would sit in the kitchen while I was preparing the feast, and we would have great discussions. I then would always hand him a bag of chocolate covered graham crackers with craisins that I stashed away just for him. He would gladly accept them with that twinkle in his eye and those deep dimples creasing his brown cheeks. He would devour most of them immediately with groans of delicious delight. I will remember him fondly as a gentle and loving person.

***

By Kristen Martini
Mary's Niece

While I didn't know him as long as everyone else, Uncle Peter made such an impact every time I did see him.

He had a twinkle in his eye that was infectious. It showed his verve for life, his enthusiasm for taking the path less traveled, his passion for surrounding himself with like-minded adventurers. He made you want to be in his circle. Annmarie, I see it in you, too.

While I'll miss him at our gatherings, I look forward to hearing the many stories I'm sure will be shared from those that loved him, and that twinkle will live on. I love you both very much.

***

The death of his mother and brother when my father was in his mid-thirties, before he had enough time to entirely repair the damage that he did, led to a disconnection with some family members who, perhaps, did not believe that he had the power to change. He continued to make the effort to mend those fractures, even decades later. His reunification with his only nephew on his side of the family was perhaps the last one that he truly wished to achieve before he died, and so it was.

***

By Philip P. Gallione, Jr.
"In Memory of Peter Gallione (Uncle Pete, my Godfather)"

I was 9 years old when I lost my father (Uncle Pete's only brother) to a heart attack. Uncle Pete (also my godfather) was the only strong adult connection I had with my father's side of the family. I never saw him, but always received a card on my Birthday and Christmas with a check for $25 and sometimes a call. Around 13, I started to grow resentful that he never came to see me or, apparently in my mind, wanted to be with me. I remember taking the check and going to the stove and saying to my mother, "I guess the checks are how he satisfies his conscience." As I watched the flame from the stove burn the check, I said, "Then this is how I will satisfy mine." After a few more cards, and a few more burnings, the cards stopped. I would not hear from my Uncle for the next 25 years.

One day, when I was around 40, my wife received a call asking if this was the home of Philip Gallione. After saying yes, he said this was his Uncle.

She texted me and asked if it was OK to give him my cell phone number. I said yes. He called and told me that he was retiring to Florida and was doing a huge family gathering before he moved. I told him that I wouldn't go to the reunion as, "not only were these people I didn't know, they were people I didn't even know of." He asked if we could do something else the next day and I said I'd consider it.

I spent a lot of time thinking about it as I knew that if I didn't see him, I likely would never reunite with him or his daughter Annmarie, who was slightly older than me but who I used to be close with as young children. I decided to have him come over and we went to I-HOP for lunch. He, Aunt Mary, Annmarie, and her two children all came to my house that Sunday. I remember when he first saw me that he was taken aback, as we were not a tall family and I was now 6'2". We had a very nice dinner and then everyone came back to the house for a while. My kids really took to him and I was happy to have a part of my father's family exposed to them.

When he moved to Florida, we would talk every couple of months or so. He would always call me on holidays, birthdays (including my Father's), etc. I know we took him out to dinner one time when he was visiting and we went to Fin in Montclair and had a nice dinner together. Another time, a few years back, we vacationed in Florida and spent a day with him at his house. Every once in a while, I would see him when he would come up to visit Annmarie. He then arranged for a huge family gathering in the Summer of 2019 where I got to meet a lot of family I never knew of. It was very nice to hear people talk so fondly about my father.

Then my life would take a turn that would connect us in a deeper way. The following week, I was at an event with a very good friend where I got intoxicated. This was not the first time she had seen me this way. Her father was an alcoholic, and she challenged me to consider if I had a bigger problem. After agreeing, the next week I attended my first AA meeting. Now, given my uncle's past, as well as what he would spend his life's work doing, we definitely had a new common topic to talk about. He provided some very good guidance to me as I worked on my recovery and, as of today (12/4/20), I have not had a drink in 514 days.

As I was out of work, in September 2020, I decided to take a road trip to see a good friend of mine in Charlotte and then go to see my Uncle in Florida. I spent about 9 days with my Uncle at his house. We played scrabble, swam in the pool, watched a lot of TV (sports, Two and a Half Men, Mom, news, and a whole lot of true crime shows). I spent 3 days helping him clean up his backyard, as he was not able to do it because of his back problems and his pending surgery.

By far the biggest thing we did was talk, as we both held a resentment toward the other. Me, for him abandoning me in my eyes, and Uncle Pete, for me not reaching out when I was older. Of course, as with everything in life, there was my side, his side, and the truth that lies somewhere in the middle. It was by far one of the most powerful amends I made in my journey and was so thankful to have had the opportunity.

The last chat I had with my Uncle, naturally, started with talking football and his beloved Giants. It was only when I spoke to Annmarie that I learned his random "I'm OK" message was after he had a heart attack in recovery. On Friday, he seemed to be getting better, and while the doctors were stressing that he needed to stay and do outpatient PT, he told me, "I am getting out of here on Saturday." These words proved to be prophetic as that would be the day he passed. The next day was my birthday, and I really missed getting the "Happy Birthday Neph, Love you" call.

I could be very guilt-ridden with the thoughts of why didn't I go to the first family reunion, why did I not do more once we reconnected, etc. etc. AA has taught me not to shut the door on the past but also not to live in it. The journey with my uncle went as it was supposed to be. I instead am grateful. Grateful that I learned I had a problem and he could provide guidance, grateful that in a COVID world I didn't find another job and had the opportunity to spend 9 quality days with my Uncle, grateful that all of the past between us was hashed out and we were just living in the present. Of course, I would wish for more time with him, but I know he is with my Dad now and that was a reunion that I am sure both were looking forward to.

***

By Eva F. Gallione

I met your father on October 14, 1963 at an Englewood/Bergenfield football game. Bergenfield won 24-0.

I ran into him as he was with your mother, Mary Martini, who was a year younger than me, but I always liked her and your grandmother. We talked and she introduced me to Peter Gallione. I was dating "Bobby" [Gallione] at that time. At that time, I was not interested in who he was or how they were related. Can't tell you anything about your dad except we talked and it was a beautiful day.

Bob and I married on September 3rd, 1967. We had so many people at our wedding, so many Galliones, nobody introduced us. But there were plenty of Galliones! When someone said to me years later "are you related to. . .", I would say, "We had many at our wedding, but I have not seen them since."

My son, Robert John Gallione Jr, graduated BHS in 1986 and my daughter Maria graduated in 1988. We knew Annmarie Gallione graduated in 1989 and she was Mary and Peter's daughter, but we didn't know how we were related, if we were even related. We didn't think about it, because we didn't know. We met Alex Gallione at political functions and were introduced to him. He looked like Bob's father, so I started to figure out that there was a connection.

Years passed, Bob's grandparents, the Galliones, died. We thought that both his paternal grandparents had no relatives. Having Ancestry, I started to check around. Years later, I finally decided to check around again. I looked on Facebook, to check out if your father was there. He was so I wrote him an email and explained the above.

Your father emailed me back and said to call him, so I did. I had my wedding list and I gave him the names of the Galliones that were there. He said, "that's my father, that's my uncle", etc. So I started to check up on Bob's DNA on Ancestry and found another connection, Karen Parille in Connecticut. I knew Bob's father visited Connecticut often. I called Karen and we determined the sibling relation between her father and Bob's grandfather. Peter called her and found out that his grandfather was another sibling. With Peter's help, and Ancestry's, we became so excited! Bobby did have family! Peter and I talked almost every day for a year until the gathering, or I emailed him every day regarding the family.

I really enjoyed your father! And I miss him! We didn't get enough time with him. We loved that he went with us to Mexico City to meet another part of our family, we loved it and we loved them! And then the Pandemic!

At the end of conversations or emails he would always say "I love you cuz!" He was so kind and gentle! And I can't tell you how much I miss him! I often asked Peter how he changed his life and how he got such a beautiful family and he told "God loves me". And I believed he did!

This is how we started the Peter Gallione Memorial Family Gathering.

***

By Robert Gallione

While Eva mentioned our high school contact with Peter, our relationship truly developed with Peter when Eva and Peter connected a few years ago as they planned for a Gallione family reunion through Ancestry. God gave us a gift by enabling us to develop our relationship as we organized the Gallione family reunion at Memorial Park, Bergenfield in 2019. Our February 2020 trip with Peter to visit our Mexico City, Mexico relatives was a special experience with him and our newfound relatives.

***

In the end, relationships were what mattered most in my father's life, and he nurtured and cherished so very many of them for many years.

***

By Ann Aschim

Pete is the only person on the planet who knew Klaus & I both before we met. In 1976, he introduced us… following his "intuition" that "this might work". He was right. Klaus and I stayed together for the rest of his life until he passed on 11/22/20, THREE WEEKS AFTER PETE. Losing the two of them in three weeks was eerie. Losing them in the alternate reality we've all survived during the pandemic has been even more difficult. Delayed funerals have delayed healing, delayed hugs, delayed a full expression of grief. I even delayed writing this, because I'm not sure I was ready to fully grieve BOTH OF THEM.

For 44 years, Pete was a constant thread in our lives. He drove us on our wedding day, he was at the hospital as soon as visitors were allowed after our daughters were born. He was a surrogate Uncle to our children. His friends were our friends and our friends were his friends. Klaus and Pete both enjoyed rather large, never-ending card games in our home. We shared many many holidays together, and if we couldn't share the entire holiday, we at least had a visit! Pete was just a part of the tapestry of our life.

Pete and Klaus both had difficult jobs providing alternatives for youth who were at dangerous risk of incarceration. They didn't always see eye-to-eye in terms of the best way to help, but they both shared a common goal: to provide opportunities for real change and keep kids from slipping through the cracks of society.

Klaus was very sick when Pete passed. The shock of the news seemed to make him numb & more distant. They had worked together, played together and were surrogate brothers to one another. They even argued like family, but they had an unconditional love for one another and a bond that couldn't be broken.

Many people have speculated about what they do on "the other side". Most people seem to project that they are doing whatever they remember as familiar to them... playing cards, hanging out with a pre-deceased friend or family member. My personal vision is that they remain strong helpers over there, as they were over here on Earth. I saw them as two men who were able to love unconditionally here. I believe love never dies, and that they have jobs over there like they did here, just without physical bodies. Helping souls transition in some way & shadowing their loved ones here like angels. Pete sometimes (okay always) found some of my views on consciousness to be "woo woo", so frankly now I smile because when I join them someday I look forward to hearing him say "YOU WERE RIGHT!" (Which he didn't say often...).

I am forever grateful to you Pete for giving me the opportunity to meet the love of my life, and please look out for him over there, just like you did here...xo

***

By Beth DiFrank

My sister and I referred to Pete as "our brother from another mother".

After his devastating loss, I started reflecting on our more than 25-year friendship and read many of the tributes people wrote on Pete's Facebook page. I realized I was not the only one that felt like Pete was family. Most of Pete's friends felt like he was also their brother from another mother, because Pete made us all feel special. He took the time and made it a priority to maintain the relationships in his life. Pete called or texted to wish us a happy birthday, happy holidays, or just to check in. He listened when we spoke and cared about what was going on in our lives.

Pete was genuine and there were no pretenses. We all knew the good, the bad and the ugly of his life which made him a unique and a very special person. We will all miss him immensely.

Love you my brother,

Your "sis", Beth

***

<u>By Barbara Ciccotelli</u>
"Petey"

"A man's man".

A phrase many have used to describe Peter Gallione, and one I debated & resisted often.

Is it that one precludes the other or, is it possible, one can additionally be a "woman's man"?

I conclude Pete was such a man.

Shortly after my husband Alfred passed, a new movie premiered called "American Pie". My daughters, aged 15 & 14 at the time, asked to see it. Knowing only its theme of senior high boys' "rites of passage", I decided it best I go along to discuss afterwards.

Wanting a male perspective, I turned to my dear friend Pete to accompany us, knowing "Uncle Pete" was the right man for this task. Not knowing it's premise & without hesitation, he agreed.

Pete knew it was important to me & always being a man true to his word, he honored his promise to be there for my girls… Alfred's girls, ALWAYS!

Well… needless to say there were many crude & sexual scenes. There was Pete, seated next to me, fidgeting, squeezing my arms, elbowing me while ADAMANTLY declaring, "I can't believe I'm watching THIS with my nieces! I'm going to kill YOU!" So Pete.

Afterwards we discussed how male teenage minds are wired, their motives & objectives. My daughters listened intently, trusting his knowledge & perspective. It was more than I had hoped. I will be eternally grateful.

For, even though it was "uncomfortable", Pete stood in the gap. He put their welfare above his own unease. Pete did this for ALL… exposing his vulnerabilities, shortcomings, & past indiscretions in an effort to LIFT others.

Be it juvenile offenders, coworkers, family, friends, or even friends of friends, Pete ALWAYS showed up to help, to counsel, to CARE.

Job well done, my friend. You touched & transformed multitudes with your love & kindness. My daughters & I were honored & privileged to be recipients.

I will forever miss your wisdom, laughter, and bear hugs.

Calls to catch up, to say merry Christmas, or to "discuss" current events.

Until we meet again… you are with me always, my dear "brother from another mother".

Your memory is a blessing.
Your "sis"
Barbara Ciccotelli

***

Because my father's true nature, when not overshadowed by drugs, was to help people, he continued working even during his retirement while in Florida. As a result, he also continued to develop new bonds with people and to share the gifts that his life journey bestowed upon him.

***

<u>By Minnie King</u>

I will never stop believing that Peter Gallione left this earth way before his time.

I remember the first time we ever spoke on the telephone. I was looking for a mental health program that could be implemented into our organization for youth offenders. Peter was listed as a co-author to the writing of a very successful, evidence-based therapeutic program. On the phone he was charming, witty, humorous, and incredibly knowledgeable. The professional chemistry was evident. I invited Peter to visit the agency. He said, "oh no, I'm retired." Two weeks later he came to the Florida Community Alliance (FCA). He looked handsome dressed in a navy blue suit, with a shiny bald scalp, clean shaven, hazel eyes and a remarkable smile. The tall, dark, and sexy type of handsome. After much convincing, Peter agreed to a short-term contract as the agencies' Clinical Director and Trainer. I felt like I won the Lottery. I had gained a clinician with more than 30 years of experience directing New Jersey's youth offender programs. And here he was at my agency. Plus, he was an expert in Rational Emotive Behavior Therapy. I prayed for an executive level leader, and Peter Gallione was an answer to my prayer.

Peter Gallione, my professional clinical partner, my mentor, my friend. He was directly responsible for the professional clinical growth of all therapists and interns at FCA. Three days a week he would drive to Palm Beach from Broward with all materials in hand. Watching him hold his lectures was magical. He simplified years of college material. He conducted his sessions with passion. "Focus on the feeling," he'd say. I would shadow his work and questioned myself on how I treated patients prior to Peter's arrival. He created an insatiable appetite for learning at FCA. He took a stagnant agency and brought it back to life. And the staff, including myself, are better at helping professionals as a result. More importantly, patients received quality and competent care. The recidivism was at an all-time low.

As my mentor and friend, we spent many afternoons on his patio drinking coffee and strategizing. His intelligence dazzled me. He shared about his struggles and successes. I shared about mine. Peter was who I reached out to for guidance during my personal crisis. When my boys experienced legal problems, Peter spent hours upon weeks upon months helping me navigate the judicial system. When I was diagnosed with cancer, Peter sat with me many times while I received my treatments. When I was arrested, Peter extended me a lifeline. There was no greater friend. He wiped my tears in one moment, while telling me to stop being such a punk the next. He was my Arc Reactor (like the one Iron Man had embedded in his chest). He made me feel invincible. He believed in me and my ability to achieve success.

A piece of me will forever feel void. Peter wasn't ready to go. I wasn't ready to lose him. Peter bragged about his life. He bragged about his daughter, grandkids, lifelong friends, his house, his garden, his pool. He even bragged about how lucky I was that he gave me the time of day. He was right. And talking shit back and forth was the way of our relationship. We argued about diagnoses, about which gender was smarter, who was more ghetto than who. I can't say who won those disagreements. I can say that they always ended in "I love you". And in him calling me a dumbass.

I miss him. The classiest man I know. The smartest man. There will never be another that even comes close. Peter, you were the best, the most talented. I aspire to one day fill your clinical shoes. I will never forget the many life lessons you taught me.

In your last text you said, "Had a heart attack, I will call you later." I wait for that call knowing that you have never broken your word to me. I always wanted you to meet my mom. Now you share space in a much better place. I know we will connect again. I love you. I miss you dearly. Thank you for everything.

***

By Terry Watson
"Remembering Pete"
Mary's close friend

I am fortunate to have been "adopted" into Pete's family and to have shared many happy times with them: great food, great fun, great warmth, and a profound love for each other.

It was during these times that I began to know Peter Gallione. I saw a man who was GENUINE — no sham, no pretense — a man who deeply loved his family, a man whose family returned that love in kind. He was a man of generous spirit who shared his life experience and knowledge to help others. That he genuinely cared about others was evident.

Knowing Pete has enriched our lives in many ways and we mourn his passing, but I believe his kind and loving spirit will always remain with us.

Rest in peace.

***

Even late in life, my father also enjoyed creating new relationships with women, while cherishing and nurturing the relationships of lovers past. I found it amusing that, after he moved to Florida, my father's second wife, Diana, with whom he remained close, routinely drove him to the airport so that he could visit us in New Jersey, where he would stay with his first wife, Mary, with whom he also remained close. While in New Jersey, my father would occasionally *"go incognito"*, as he called it, and for a day or so we didn't ask where he was or what he was doing. We didn't have to ask, because we knew, and we understood.

***

By Nica Spalletta

I met Pete on Match.com close to 14 years ago. We would talk on the phone almost every day. He helped me understand what my son was going through with his addiction. We talked also about when we would get together and meet; we got along so well on the phone, it was the next step. Our phone friendship went on for a long time until Pete told me he was going to be relocating to Florida, and before he left he wanted to meet me. I was so happy that this man with whom I had a great connection was finally coming to North Jersey to meet. He came to my home, rang the bell, I was a little nervous, but when I saw him at my door I just smiled and we hugged. It was like home.

We went to dinner and just had a great time. He took me home and told me the next day that he would be moving to Florida, and that now he was sorry that we didn't get together sooner. I was sad because we had such a great connection. Well, Pete moved and our phone conversations continued on a daily basis for years, and he would say that there is a reason that for all these years we just stayed in touch.

Pete knew my fear of flying but he kept asking me to fly down to Florida. Finally, this year we decided that I was coming down to Florida after the Pandemic with my daughter and granddaughter, who had both come to love him as I did. He was so happy to be going for the surgery, he would finally be rid of the daily pain. He wanted everything in order for his daughter Annmarie in case something should happen. I told him he was going to be fine, not to worry, and that I was looking forward to seeing him.

My daughter and granddaughter live with me and it gets crazy sometimes, so I completely forgot to call Pete and wish him good luck and to tell him all was going to be ok. I texted him when I finally realized that it was the day of the surgery. It was Tuesday, October 27, and I told him I was so sorry that I didn't get to speak with him but that he was in my thoughts and prayers and he is going to be fine and that I loved him.

On Wednesday, October 28, I got a text from Pete saying, "Ok. Don't get nuts. I'm ok but had a heart attack after the surgery. I'm Ok. In ICU..will explain over the weekend." Well, I did go nuts, but I told him I wasn't and that he was in my thoughts and prayers. He texted me back with just a heart which I will keep forever and I told him to just relax and listen to the doctors and he gave me a thumbs up. On Sunday, November 1 at 10:30 p.m., I texted Pete again "I've been waiting to hear from you..I don't want to bother you I hope everything is OK".

On November 2 at 8:32 a.m., I received a text from Pete's phone, but it wasn't Pete. It was Annmarie letting me know that he had passed away. I couldn't believe that he was gone. I miss you so much. I will never forget you. I truly loved Pete with all my heart. He loved to hear me sing the song "At Last". He is on my mind everyday. I'm so blessed to have had him in my life. Thank you Pete, for your time, your friendship, and your love... You are forever in my heart! We will most definitely meet again!

***

By Anonymous

Annmarie, you were as close to your father as any two special persons can be. He shared everything with you. You know your dad and women. He was irresistible.

One day, he walked over to me while I was whining about a setback and he kissed me. Then he said, "Now, shut the fuck up and let's go to lunch." From that point on, I was smitten. I will leave it at that.

I join you in missing him. So glad he got his last wish and Biden won. Keep being good to yourself. A dad would never want more for his daughter than that. He used to share how you taught him to be a dad by being a badass and holding him accountable for his shit. Amazing doesn't wear off. Keep being amazing.

***

My father knew how to talk to people. He knew when to push and (most of the time) when to back off. He was an effective communicator, and expected those in his presence to communicate back with him effectively. He challenged people in their thinking and sometimes infuriated them, while at the same time endearing them to him. If you knew my father, then you knew his "way" and how damn persuasive he could be in the coolest way possible.

If I had a dime for every time my father remarked, "*Ok. Why?*", I would be a lot wealthier than I am now. Even an explanation of "why" led to him responding, again, "*Yes, but why?*", and so on, causing his counterpart to continuously go deeper into her or his thinking. "*Getting to the root*" of things was a favorite pastime of my father's. Why? Because you couldn't arrive at a solution without first ascertaining the problem. In the simplest terms, my layperson theory is that this is why my father never relapsed after his recovery and why he was successful at what he did for a living and in his personal relationships. It is also why so many people enjoyed talking to him and found counsel in him.

Throughout his lifetime, my father was asked by several people to be the godfather to their children. He also devoted an extensive amount of time and energy into raising Diana's three nephews, Guy, Lance and Michael, and they remained close with him until the very end. Despite his history, which he did not hide, people trusted him. He not only had a way of connecting with youth from all different walks of life as a result of his professional life, but he could also be counted on by them in his personal life.

***

By Toni Marie Berry
My father's goddaughter

Thanks to my parents, my life started with the best-chosen godparents in the whole world, my Uncle Pete and my Aunt Diana. I can still remember the sounds of their beautiful, sweet, sweet voices when I was little and the pure excitement that filled me when I knew they were stopping by. Although, I heard that when they babysat me once, I screamed my head off. I must have driven him to smoke that day.

I was born in 1983, three years after he and Aunt Diana were married. I remember visiting them at their home in Terrestria. They had Tara, his beautiful long-haired German Shepherd, who he absolutely adored.

And oh my god, Aunt Diana's birds, which Uncle Pete hated.

He never missed a birthday and I always got the sweetest cards from my beautiful godparents every year. I'll always cherish the gift of the big, stuffed giraffe, which I named Petey, after him. It was so special to me. It gave me a lot of comfort and love when I needed it most, just like my Uncle Pete did.

He was always there for me with so much love and support and guidance. As I got older, I don't know how Uncle Pete would know I was in need of help, but he would just show up like a magical godfather whenever I deeply needed it, and he always had the right words. It was like an intuition he had. He gave me so much strength when I needed it, and in this absolute, selfless, superhero way he would be there for me in the blink of an eye.

I remember calling him whenever I needed to talk. His voice was just so loving. It was such a comfort to me in trying times and I miss it so much. He always made me feel loved, he really did. It's hard to write about the amount of light and love that he brought to me.

When Uncle Pete lived in Florida, I sent him Jersey tomatoes each summer because he loved them so much. He was always so grateful, and I know he enjoyed them because he told me all about how delicious they were and even posted on Facebook about it.

Uncle Pete was just so therapeutic, and I think it was that way for everyone. I remember calling him one time when I just needed to cry and he just let me. He talked to me and everything was just better.

His death is awful, but it has connected me and Annmarie and for that I am grateful. Whenever we talk about Uncle Pete, we both know exactly what we mean. I told Annmarie that I will be here for her day or night just like her dad offered to me. Except during nap time, haha. Everyone knows about Uncle Pete's nap times.

He was the best person in the entire world. I've never met anyone in the whole entire world like him, and I was so blessed to have him as my godfather.

***

By Donna Marie Alexander

I first met Pete and Diana when we became neighbors at LaCascata. We quickly became best friends. Loved our game nights and Pete's obsession with Yahtzee. The competitive rivalry during sports games between the husbands was serious for them, but funny to me and Diana. My husband was Philly teams all the way, and of course Pete was a devout New York fan. The good times and funny calamities with our dogs are too many to mention, but those memories will always be with me.

When Pete and Diana decided to tie the knot, my husband Rudy and I were witnesses at their marriage.

So of course it was only fitting that when our first child Toni was born, we asked them to be her godparents.

Through the years Pete was always there for me, giving advice or just being uplifting. I will always love him as family and will miss him dearly.

***

My father enjoyed playing sports, cards, and word games immensely. I never met anyone who could beat him at a game of Boggle, which was infuriating, especially as I developed a deep love of words throughout my lifetime. I have no idea how many Words with Friends games he had going but I promise you, it was a lot! Some of the most uplifting aspects of my father's letters from jail were when he reported to us on how his softball or baseball team did, how banged up he got in the process, or how he was looking forward to watching the Ali-Foreman fight. Playing sports made my father feel free, and that was a feeling that he lost for a while.

Healthy competition was so much a part of who he was (including a bit of incessant trash talking) and he made games fun. He had a way of good-naturedly insulting you while simultaneously cracking you up. He was a humble winner and a funny loser. And, as much as he talked trash, he complimented and lifted those around him up in the most genuine way possible all of the time, even strangers. I couldn't even go for a walk around the Paintworks with my dad without him enamoring some person or creature. There is a good story that I'm not willing to put into print, but which I might tell if asked about the time that my dad and I met that nice lady on our walk around Silver Lake. Ask me sometime.

For as much as he loved being competitive in his own right, there were few things that gave my father more of a thrill than watching me play sports. He used to say that even though he only had one child, he got one of each in me. I can still hear his voice in the stands and see his look from across the court when I got pulled from the game once again for getting into foul trouble.

Top: Nancy Martini, Tom Scott, Ed Martini, Michelle Scott;
Bottom: Michael Fiore, Anna Martini, Peter Gallione

My father continued to be one of my biggest fans into my forties, even coming to cheer on my softball team when he visited from his home in Florida. A few years ago, when I started playing again, I restrung the softball glove that he played with for many years, and I still use it to this day. His unwavering support of me throughout my life, both on the playing field and off of it, is something that I think of each and every time I slide my hand inside of the glove that used to catch balls sent his way and now serves the same purpose for me.

Living in South Jersey for much of his adult life, but being a New York sports fan, made for some interesting interactions between my father and people in his community. He enjoyed going to Phillies-Mets games in his New York garb. He was the type of baseball fan that watched all year, not just postseason games. He stuck by his Mets, year after year, even as they struggled for so long.

My father was not quiet about his political views, but this rarely dissuaded people from conversing with him about them. Maybe it was his smile or maybe it was the way that he made you feel valued as a person, even when you disagreed with him. He was a Democrat, partially because he learned firsthand what good government programs can do for people and, therefore, he supported the expansion and refinement of those programs. He also cared about others as much, if not more than, he cared about himself in his later years.

My father advocated strongly for racial justice, which was a tremendous part of his belief that drugs — all drugs — should be legal. Yet another book could be written about the underlying rationale for my father's arguments in favor of a total reform of national and state drug policies. He had many reasons, all of them good:

- ❖ Our jails are full of drug offenders;
- ❖ Treatment requires a large amount of funding and what better source than legalization and taxation;
- ❖ Alcohol is a more dangerous drug and our laws are inconsistent;
- ❖ Criminalization does not deter;
- ❖ Our policies have a disproportionate effect on minority populations;
- ❖ And many others.

Personally, he had me convinced the first time we talked about it, and he got most other people on board when he discussed it. The only reason not to legalize drugs, in his opinion, was because he felt that it would take a whole industry away from some communities and those who were displaced would turn to robberies and other violent conduct, so crime would be raised in those areas.

My father was proud of his country in many ways and greatly respected those who served it. 9/11 hit him hard, as it did so many. He worked on the side of the State for so long that he most definitely came to respect women and men in uniform. His brother was a Marine and his parents were highly respectful of authority. He was *not* proud of the fact that his victims on August 9, 1973 had turned out to be law enforcement officers. He had thought they were just thug dealers and it weighed on his mind that he had gone so far off the deep end that he put a gun to one of "the good guys'" heads. It weighed on my mind, too, so I googled Detective Asmuss and learned that he was adjudicated liable in a civil matter for a false arrest and police brutality incident, so then it weighed on my mind less. When I administered my father's estate, I learned that he was a regular contributor to the Police Benevolent Association. He had never mentioned that to me, and I think it was his way of doing a small, silent penance over the years in addition to his other tremendous service to the community.

With the exception of Donald Trump, my father could usually find a good quality in any person. Indeed, he dealt with many people who had done wrong in their lives and he was a mastermind at helping many of them find self-love and forgiveness so that they could carry on and right those wrongs. It is no secret that, in my father's mind, Donald Trump was a dangerous mistake of a man who possessed none of the characteristics of a decent human being. He used to joke (we think) that if there ever was an attempted assassination, the Secret Service would *"come to my house first"*.

And yet, my father maintained close relationships with many people who disagreed with him on this and other matters of public concern. Some of his closest friends were people with wildly different worldviews than him. He continuously engaged people in their manner of thinking and tried, in as healthy of a way as he could muster, to have meaningful conversations with them. Whereas, in his early life his tendency was to escalate conflict, in his later life, he was a pro at de-escalating it. He was truthful and direct but respectful, also. And people just loved being around him and talking to him.

***

By Lisa Parisi
"Thoughts of my Uncle Pete"
Peter's Niece

I think it was winter 1989, but I am terrible with dates. I was dating Guy, Uncle Pete's nephew, and we lived in South Florida. I had a career at the time working for Delta Airline Vacations as a Business Development Rep and part of my territory was Philadelphia and the surrounding NJ area. As my business trip to Philly/South Jersey arose, it was suggested that I visit (and meet for the first time, by myself), Aunt Diane, Uncle Pete, and family! So, being the Jersey girl I am, I knocked on their door that cold winter day, and we became family.

We had so many memorable and fun times as an extended family, from playing cards and board games over Christmas holidays to dancing non-stop at our wedding, which Uncle Pete was part of. The most heartwarming thing about Uncle Pete is that he was always there for you. Whether it was a quick, "Happy Birthday" call, a heartfelt Christmas card in the mail, or a Facebook exchange on the state of the NY Giants!

I really loved seeing him and my dad, Joe, banter back and forth about football, politics, or whatever. Even though they were opposites on their political views, they laughed, bantered, and argued, and it couldn't be more fun. We spent a few Sundays in recent years watching the NY Giants. Win or lose, these were special times. Don't forget the Mountain Dew, Uncle Pete will be there!

We all have ups and downs in our lives, and Uncle Pete was there in good times and bad. He never judged, he always listened, and never had a bad word about anyone. I honestly don't think I saw him ever get mad.

Uncle Pete was a special guy. He will be so missed. I was grateful that he was the confirmation Godfather for my son, Joey. He was always there to lend a guiding word of encouragement. He attended his football games and really took a genuine interest in whatever was going on in all of our busy lives. He was a true role model for all those whose lives he touched. It doesn't seem real he is gone. I know he is looking down at us and is at peace, and that brings me great comfort.

Thank you, Annmarie, for the opportunity to share. You were truly the apple of his eye!

***

By Rick Frank

I knew your Dad through his friendship with Klaus. I never had the opportunity to work with him or really spend enough time with him. It was just a few moments here and there at meetings through the years. But a good friendship developed in the process and we enjoyed each other's company. Your Dad always had a joyful smile, a supportive hug, and a willingness to listen — or challenge you a bit when you needed it. He was laser-focused when you needed to tap into his years of wisdom and experience.

There is no single memory that stands out, just a beautiful series of encounters through the years. Your speech at his retirement was very moving for me. And then Pete and I connected on Facebook and shared a good amount of laughs and stories. He would post a picture of that awesome pool in the dead of winter just to taunt us up here in New Jersey, and I remember going back in forth with him about New Jersey vs. Florida with lines like "at least I can work in my garden without worrying about an alligator sneaking up on my ass."

In the last few years, we shared a disdain for Trump and a fascination with Kamala Harris (yes, he had an obvious crush on her). After helping each other get through the last four years in politics, I was greatly looking forward to sharing the victory and the healing of our country in the coming years. I miss those almost daily exchanges. Your Dad was a great, great man. He deeply cared about the juveniles we worked with and equally about those of us who were fortunate to be his friend.

Sending hugs and love to you, Annmarie. I hope that things are leveling off a bit for you and your family, and you know how much your Dad was loved and respected by many.

***

The posthumous notes of congratulations to my father following the 2020 presidential election were incredibly heartwarming. So many knew of my father's wish for the outcome of that historic contest and, though sharing it with him would have been so enjoyable, we take solace in the fact that his unwavering support helped to elevate the first woman in our nation's history to the position of Vice-President. That would have made him so very happy.

My father's retirement to Florida brought about his era of simplicity and peace, something that he had worked extremely hard to achieve through his active lifetime. I often asked him if he was beginning to get bored and his response was *"not even a little bit."* He woke up each morning in a home that he loved, thanked his god for allowing him another wakeup, got his coffee and his cigarette, took a dip in his pool, and listened to the sounds of nature and his waterfall. He watched news, sports, and his favorite shows on television, which he could see from that very pool.

Throughout the day, there would be phone calls, lots of them, and visits with loved ones. He lived alone, but my father was not, by any stretch of the imagination, a lonely man. He traveled a good bit, and it was usually to visit family.

It is true what these essays reflect — my father never missed the opportunity to wish someone he cared about a happy birthday nor did he usually forget momentous occasions like an anniversary of the loss of a loved one. He wrote the most thoughtful and heartfelt messages in cards, in that ridiculously beautiful penmanship that he possessed. We traveled to Florida a few times each year to spend uninterrupted time with him and he came home to New Jersey every June and every December for extended periods of time to celebrate birthdays, Father's Day, and Christmas. When his granddaughter published her first book at the age of 16, he was there, front and center, beaming with happiness and pride for her accomplishment. Likewise, he did the same for me when I opened my own business. He was there for us, always.

On various birthdays, my children were gifted solo trips to Florida with "Poppi" to spend one-on-one time with him. The joy in my father's heart during these times was obvious, and he always expressed it, as he was wont to do. He took those opportunities to truly connect with his grandchildren, and to impart whatever words of wisdom that he could to them.

***

By Nathaniel Jensen

Poppi was, and always will be, one of the greatest people I ever had the pleasure to know. Not only was he a kind and fun-loving human, but a caring and thoughtful grandfather too. While I only knew him towards the end of his life, I cherished the moments I had with him. From splitting open coconuts in his backyard to taking a road trip from Jersey to Florida, every memory is one I will always keep with me.

I never knew my grandfather when he was a young and reckless teenager. From what my mom and grandma have told me, I can only assume he was a good kid who made some bad choices. Fortunately for him and us, he turned it all around and lived a good and giving life in the end. But I would still love to have a one-on-one conversation with 17 year-old Pete Gallione. Wouldn't that be fun?

When I think of mentors in my life, Poppi is always one of them in my mind. Not just that he taught me how to punch when I was 9, or trained me to never respond with "yeah, but...". It was the way he engaged in conversation, always having something interesting to say and always listening like he's interested. Even when I would rant about superheroes or movies, he always looked at me like it was the most important thing in the world. That may have been because we were the most important thing in his world.

While I wish I had more time with him, I cherish the experiences that proved to me how much of an amazing father, grandfather, mentor, and friend he really was. Although he isn't with us anymore, I know that he would be very proud of my accomplishments and would especially have liked to meet my girlfriend. My grandfather was one of those special humans you just don't get to meet another of.

***

<u>*By Eve Jensen*</u>

I remember being about five years old in a hotel room. I'm not sure where it was, or why we were there, but I remember being very young and very hot. My parents were upset with me for something — likely something my fault, but I certainly didn't see it that way. I ran into the adjoining room, where my Poppi, Peter, was sitting on a small loveseat. I jumped into his arms and wrapped my own around his neck. My parents came in, silent, and Poppi chuckled. I myself suppressed a smile where my head was buried in his chest. He knew the same thing I did: they wouldn't dare yell at me while I was in his arms.

I went running to him in that moment because he made me feel safe, always. About a decade later, when my mental health was on the decline and I didn't particularly feel like talking to anyone about it, he came running to me.

We sat and talked for a long time. He tried to help me understand exactly what I was feeling and where it might have been coming from. He hit me with that "Yes, but why?" spiral he was fond of, and it was infuriating. I inherited his contentious nature and hated having circles run around me. Especially once I realized there was a teeny, tiny chance he might be right.

It was a process I knew even then he had probably gone through hundreds of times with the people he treated, and likely even more time with himself. He explained to me that no one could make me feel anything, as my emotions were my own to control and could not be dominated by outside influences. I could not control what other people did; I could only control my response and my reaction to it. In this, there was a lot of power, he tried to convince me.

He reiterated this to me in a letter he wrote in the spring of my freshman year of high school, which was to be opened by me 4 years later upon my graduation.

Most importantly, remember what I have been trying to drill into you and by now you would have gotten it. No one and no event 'can make you feel anything'. And, it's not that you 'allow' them to make you feel something/anything. Your feelings are yours; they come from inside you as you perceive the world around you and how you process and value what you are experiencing. If I could instill one meaningful skill in you, it would be that. Be empowered and never an emotional victim.

I didn't fully understand what he was saying back then. It seemed ludicrous, and scary. It was terrifying to think that I was in complete control of my own feelings, as then there would be no one else to blame. I'm still not sure if I fully understand it, but I know that trying to puzzle it out has given me a much deeper understanding of my own mind and has helped me become a better and happier person.

In that letter, my grandfather gave me a few other pieces of advice that he thought I should follow as I entered adulthood. If I could send him a letter in the afterlife, I think it would go something like this:

Dear Poppi,

Thank you for your letter. It was beautifully-written. I know how much you always wanted to be a writer, and I think that I may have inherited my own love of writing partially from you.

I promise to try to live each day centered on love, appreciation, and gratitude, just like you encouraged me. I will remember that life will bring me challenges and, with each one, a chance to grow. Even though it's not always easy, I will try to be resilient and resolved. Since you asked, I will be kind to others and to myself. I won't feel entitled, I will work hard, and be focused and patient. I hope that you are right and that wonderful surprises will be mine.

You have brightened my life too, Poppi, ever since June 25, 2001. Thank you for always lifting me higher and believing in me.

Love you to the end of the universe and back again, too.

Love, Evie

***

My own one-on-one time with my father during his retirement in Florida consisted of many long telephone conversations and as many visits as we could muster. He was my first call whenever I had to make a drive of any distance and our conversations were always worth it. I hated talking on the phone, but not with him. We were both active on social media, so he used to say he could just check Facebook to see where I was and what I was up to.

My father knew and understood me deeply, likely better than any other person has ever known or understood me in my life. I especially enjoyed our long drives back to Florida after he would visit us in New Jersey for the holidays. The journey held us captive to one another for a straight 20ish hours, and so the conversations got extremely raw and honest. By the time we got to South Florida, we were both delirious and spent and, for us, that meant that everything was funny. The exhaustion turned into giddiness and silliness. Our backs would hurt (his more than mine), and we couldn't wait to get to his house, but it never caused us to be in a bad mood. It took a lot to put my father in a bad mood, in my estimation.

There is so much more to say about him, but I'll never be able to tell it all. He loved his nice cars, sunsets and R&B and jazz music. He was fiercely independent. For most of his years living in Florida, he preferred to drive up and back rather than fly, so that he could have his car with him at all times (and could hit the road whenever he wished). His laugh was thoroughly contagious. He never went anywhere without his WaWa coffee and his Werthers. This past Christmas, our first without him, I asked the members of our family to all enjoy one of those delicious hard candies in his honor and to reflect upon their relationship with him as they did. Maybe next year, we'll smoke a pack of Kools.

The dogs in my father's life were family to him and were treated like gold. He had a way with them like no other. Our own dogs, Tanner and Jackson, could go months without seeing him and would then literally go berserk as he parked his car and approached our house. Their eyes would lock, the dog would wag his tail so furiously that he nearly fell over and that massive, dimpled, smile of my father's would emerge on his face. They were clearly enamored with one another and it was a sight to behold.

***

"By" Tara, Boca, Nika, Maya, Jackson, Tanner and the Hondos

Thank you for being our human and grandhuman. We don't know how we got so lucky. We will never forget the way you would look at us, pet us, and talk to us. When we heard your voice, it made us so, so happy. Thank you for all of the kisses. You gave us more attention and more treats than anyone else and took such good care of us.

> *We hope that we added to your life the way that you added to each of ours. (We kind of know we did, because it was no secret how much you loved us.) Sometimes we overheard people say that you loved dogs more than you loved humans. We believe it. And you loved humans a lot, so that must mean that you* <u>really</u> *loved us.*

> *Some of us have been waiting for you over the rainbow bridge. Two of us will "see you when I see you", just like you used to say.*

***

Our last visit with my father was in June of 2020, during the COVID-19 pandemic, and a few months before the back surgery that ultimately became too much for his heart. If heaven is anything like my father's utopia, the spirits of each of those beautiful pups are right there beside him. The last picture that I have of me and my father was on Father's Day 2020, and I now write these final words about him on Father's Day 2021, my first ever without him since his incarceration.

During quarantine, my father joked repeatedly about the fact that it was the "best bid" he ever did. He had his pool (they didn't have those in prison), his own TV (and he didn't have to vote with other inmates on which show would get played), his own phone (and he got more than 25 minutes a week on it), his tablet, his coffee, and his cigarettes. I used to worry that being alone would bring back too many difficult memories for him of his time in prison. But, he was not alone. My father had the good fortune to be surrounded, in one way or another, with plenty of family and friends who loved him and who cherished their relationships with him, and this made his life complete.

People have asked me whether it was hard for me to share my father with so many other people. It wasn't. I learned the value of relationships from him and, if I am to be completely honest, there was never an inkling of a doubt in my mind that I came first.

My father did not expect to live to be the age that he did. Because of this, he was eternally grateful for each day. He began each and every day after he overcame his addiction with a *"thank you"*. He then put his feet on the floor, turned off his fan, and proceeded to live a life that was worthy and meaningful day after day until the one when he left this earthly realm.

***

AFTERWORD
By Annmarie and Peter Gallione

The mind works in mysterious ways, my father often said. Fortunately for him, and for those who knew him, he appreciated the study of it and devoted much of his life to trying to understand it. He often talked about writing a book in order to help teenagers cope better and to ease their emotional burdens, whatever those may be. He believed strongly that the answer to so many quality-of-life issues for adolescents was found in managing their emotions.

After his death, I discovered a file on his computer drive entitled, simply, Introduction to Book. The contents contained many of the things that my father tried to teach me, my children, and many others who he encountered throughout his lifetime.

INTRODUCTION
By Peter Gallione

When my granddaughter turned 13 and my grandson turned 10, I wondered what their journey through adolescence would look like. What would they discover in the day-to-day events unfolding in their lives? I believe that the most important aspect of their experiences would be their thoughts and feelings about the world that is opening up to them. So, I decided to write this book.

I worked in the field of substance abuse for over 30 years; 20 of which was working with adolescents. I retired in 2007 as the Substance Abuse Administrator for New Jersey's Juvenile Justice Commission. What an incredible and rewarding career. What I discovered was that teenagers, despite their varied cultures, environments, the different generations and experiences, were no different from the teens of the past. I think that many people might disagree with that statement and that will stimulate some very interesting conversation. However, I found what most young people today still value the most is to feel loved and cared for, feel safe, accepted and valued, discover who they are and where they fit in with others their age, and more freedom and independence.

Through research, interviews with youth, and discussions with other professionals, as well as my own personal and professional background, I will highlight what issues are important to youth. Specifically, I will talk at length about teenage "feelings". Not enough time, energy, and importance is focused on this issue, yet is it the most vital aspect of their adventure.

Feelings have a powerful influence over alcohol and other substance use and abuse, bullying, suicide, peer pressure and the response to peer pressure, sense of themselves, self-esteem and self-image, confidence, motivation, and decision making. Yes, it's true for people of any age, but adolescence is a unique time of their lives.

I hope that this book will be the impetus for teens to discuss their feelings with parents, guardians, teachers, professionals, and most importantly, each other. Additionally, I hope this book can be used by adults to open the door to conversations with youth.

I will write as if I'm speaking directly to youth.

I acknowledge the contributions made by Ronald Jensen, Wayne Poppalardo, Janet Laufenburg, and Paul Alton.

Special acknowledgement to my daughter Annmarie, granddaughter Evie, and grandson Nate and I dedicate this book to them.

***

We dedicate this book to you, Dad. Thank you for creating a life that had such a deep and profound impact on so many and one that is worthy of re-telling. Your story is now written.